MY PETS

Real Happenings in My Aviary

Nadakkavu, Kozhikode, Kerala, 673011
www.insightpublica.com
e-mail: insightpublica@gmail.com

Title: MY PETS Real Happenings in My Aviary
Author: **Marshall Saunders**
First Insight Edition: June2024
Copyright © Reserved
All rights reserved.
Printed and Published by
InsightinPublica Printers & Publishers Pvt. Ltd.
ISBN 9789355177216
₹324

MY PETS

Real Happenings in My Aviary

Marshall Saunders

Contents

CHAPTER I

THE STORY OF TWO OWLS

The birds that really started me in the serious, and yet amusing task of keeping an aviary, were two little Californian screech owls.

The year was 1899, and I was studying boy life in the charming Belmont School, twenty-five miles from San Francisco. The grounds of the school lie on the lower slope of hills that enclose an open valley fronting the bay of San Francisco. A walk of twelve miles took us to the shores of the Pacific. Close to the school were beautiful cañons that the boys and older persons were never tired of exploring. The lads of the school were allowed to keep dogs, horses, pigeons, poultry—indeed, any pets they chose to have. One day, when I was up in the poultry yard, where there were some choice bantams and game-fowl, I saw a boy trotting about with a box in his hand.

"What have you there?" I asked.

"Four little owls," he replied. "I got them the other day when I was out walking, and I had their mother too, but she has flown away."

"What are you going to do with them?" I said.

"I don't know," he replied thoughtfully. "I don't want to bother with them. I suppose it would be best to kill them."

I looked in the box. Those four solemn-eyed, motherless balls of down appealed to me. In southern California I had been very much taken with the little owls that sat on hillocks, and turned their heads round and round to look after any one riding or driving by, until it really seemed as if they would twist them off.

I felt that I must adopt these little Northerners, so I said to the boy, "I will take them."

He joyfully resigned his charges, for he did not like the idea of destroying them, and I thoughtfully pursued my way to my room; what did owls eat?

I asked everybody I met, and the universal recommendation was, "Give them raw meat. That is the best substitute for the birds, mice, and insects that their parents catch for them."

I went to the Japanese cook, and with a friendly grin he seized a huge knife and swung himself down the hill to the meat-room.

On receiving a piece of beef, I minced it fine, and dropped small morsels into the open beaks of my new pets. They were hungry, and after eating, nestled down together and went to sleep.

The days are mild, but the nights are chilly about the bay of San Francisco. So after their latest supper, I put a rubber bag of hot water under their nest and covered them up for the night.

In the morning I hurried to their basket, and uncovered the nest I had made for them. They were as warm as toast, and four wide-open beaks pleaded eloquently for food. I cut up more meat, and for days fed them when hungry, and carried them out of doors in the sunshine, where they were objects of interest to every one about the place, especially to the dogs that would fain have devoured them.

One Sierra collie dog, Teddy Roosevelt by name, in whose upbringing I was assisting, used to tremble as he stared at them, partly from jealousy, partly because he recognized lawful prey in them.

One day some one suggested gopher—that is, ground-squirrel meat—as a change of diet. The gophers do an immense amount of damage in California on lawns and in flower-gardens, where they burrow to get at the tender roots.

I went to a house near by, where a gentleman was trying to get rid of the gophers that were devastating his lawn. He put up a warning hand when he saw me coming. A line of hose lay beside him, with which he had been trying to flood a gopher out of his hole. Presently the poor little fellow came struggling up. The gentleman despatched him with a satisfied, "He is the last one. Now the grass will grow."

He presented me with the dead body, and animated by a feeling of duty to my owl family, I carried it home, cut off a piece, and offered it to the owls. They would not eat it. They preferred mutton, beef, or veal. On these they flourished.

Soon I had another meat-eating bird given to me. While walking in a beautiful cañon, where live-oaks and ferns, green from spring rains, abounded, one of the teachers who had strayed from the rest of the party, came back to us with a young sparrowhawk that he had found. No parents seemed to be near. If left on the ground it would perish. In the light of subsequent experience, I would have put it high up on a branch and left it, trusting to the parents to find it. At that time I did not understand how faithful and constant birds are in following their young, so I took it in spite of its dismal squawks, and carried it back to the school.

My owls, by this time, had grown famously, and like children, they began to exercise their tiny limbs. It was very amusing to see them trying to climb from the center of their box to the top. They would stretch out diminutive claws, mount over each other, fall back, try again, and finally succeeded in sitting all in a row on the top, looking with solemn, questioning eyes on the great world around them. I put Hawkie with them, and they adopted him as a brother, and usually kept him in the middle. It was a pretty sight to see the row of five, with the mottled, brown bird tucked snugly between his owl friends.

When the summer vacation came, and the boys dispersed,

I went with some friends to live in a cottage across the bay of San Francisco, just under the slope of Mount Tamalpais. At the back of the cottage was a veranda shaded by a climbing rose. In the rose branches I put Hawkie and my two owls, named Solomon and Betsy.

Very regretfully I had been obliged to part from two of the little owls, for the boy who had given them to me was so pleased with the progress they had made, that he asked for the return of a part of his gift. I was sorry afterward that he had not let me keep them, for a cat soon made away with them. As the summer went by, I wondered that I did not lose my three pets. They sat all day long in the rose branches. Daytime, of course, is sleepy time for owls, but even when dusk came on they made no attempt to fly away, and the hawk only made one or two half-hearted efforts to fly across the garden out into the road.

Toward autumn the owls were fully developed, and other little screech owls had found them out, and at dusk would come about the cottage, saying softly, "Too, who, who, who, who!"

Solomon and Betsy never seemed interested enough to respond, and every evening I took them in the house where Hawkie went to sleep, and Betsy and Solomon became lively, and in the gentlest and sweetest of tones hooted for their meat.

They were tiny creatures, their bodies being not much larger than a New England robin's, but their eyes seemed immense. They had a peculiar habit of staring at their food, then twisting their heads round and round before they pounced on it. It was very amusing to see the owls "focus," and it became a way of entertaining our friends.

They often had a tug of war over their meat, when I gave it to them without cutting it up. Sollie would seize one end of a piece of beefsteak, and Betsy would grasp the other, and then they would brace their little claws and pull until the taste of the raw flesh being too tantalizing, one would let go to swallow a morsel, and at once lose the whole thing.

When the autumn had come we, with other summer residents, left Mill Valley where, I must not forget to say, numbers of beautiful birds abounded. Some of the public-spirited citizens had imported foreign birds in the hope of acclimating them. I was often awakened by a gay note and a flash of red at the window, as some foreigner wished me good-morning. The birds were protected, and the fine forests were also protected. When we went for picnics, mounted guards would warn us that we must light no fires under the magnificent old trees.

The owl's next place of residence was Berkeley, where my younger sister went to take classes in the State University. We had rented a small cottage there, and to this day we laugh over our experiences in moving to our new home. We had the two owls, Hawkie, the dog Teddy, and a chipmunk that my married sister had brought me from Lake Tahoe, that most beautiful of Californian summer resorts. How were we to take charge of all these creatures? For we had to cross the bay of San Francisco, then recross it to Berkeley. We finally got a large cage for Hawkie and the owls, and put in a compartment, giving them the upper part, and the chipmunk the lower. The dog we put on a chain.

Taking the train from Mill Valley to Sausalito, we boarded the steamer for San Francisco, changed to another, and went across the bay to Oakland, thence by train to Berkeley. When we arrived there it was late in the afternoon, and my sister and I, the dog, the owls, Hawkie, and the chipmunk, were all tired out. Indeed, the dog, who was very petted and spoiled, and who did not enjoy traveling, had dark rings around his eyes, and was in a peevish, mischievous condition. To my sister's disgust, for she being the younger was the victim, he started to run away. She had to run after him, and came back exhausted.

To add to our troubles, we could not get into our cottage that night. Fortunately, our landlady took boarders, and offered us a room in her house. We gladly accepted this offer, and putting the subdued Teddy in a tool-shed, took the birds in the house.

My sister says she never was more tired in her life than she was that night. We were sleeping blissfully, when we were awakened by a well-known sound. The naughty little owls, glad of the peace and quietness of the night after the turmoil of the day, were hooting persistently and melodiously.

"The landlady and the boarders," gasped my sister; "they will hear and wake up. Can't you stop the little wretches?"

I sprang out of bed, and addressed a solemn remonstrance to Solomon and Betsy. They were exceedingly glad to see me, and distending their little throats, continued to hoot, their clear, sweet young voices carrying only too well on the still Californian night air.

Then the chipmunk woke up and began to slide up and down an inclined piece of wood in his part of the cage. We were in despair. We could not sleep, until I had the happy thought of giving the owls a bath. I seized Betsy, held her in a basin of water, and wet her feathers considerably. Then I served Solomon in the same way, and for the rest of the night the tiny little things occupied themselves in smoothing their wet plumage. The chipmunk quieted down, and we had peace.

When we got into the cottage I had a carpenter build a small aviary at the back of it, with a box for rainy weather. The nights were not too cold for my hardy birds. Indeed, they were not too cold for many semi-tropical ones. I found a bird fancier not far from me, who had built a good-sized, open-air aviary, where he kept canaries and foreign finches all the year round, with only a partly open, glass shelter for the birds to use when it rained.

My sparrowhawk did not seem unhappy in my aviary, but

he never had the contented, comfortable expression that the owls had. His apathy was pathetic, and the expression of his beautiful, cruel eyes was an unsatisfied one. In time, I should have allowed him to go, but suddenly he fell ill. I think I overfed him, for I got him into the habit of taking a late supper, always leaning out the window and handing him a piece of meat on the end of a stick before I went to bed.

I brought him into the warm kitchen, where he moped about for a few days. Just before he died he came hopping toward the parlor, where I sat entertaining a friend. I often took him in there on the broad windowsill and talked to him as I sat sewing.

He stood in the doorway, gave me a peculiar look, as if to say, "I would come in if you were alone," hopped back to the kitchen, and in a short time was no more.

My sister and I mourned sincerely for our pretty bird, and I had the uncomfortable feeling that I might have done better if I had left him in his own habitat—but then he might have starved to death if his parents had not found him. Would death by starvation have been any more painful than his death with me? Possibly some larger creature might have killed him swiftly and mercifully—it was a puzzling case, and I resolved to give up worrying about it. I had done what I considered was best, and I tried to console myself for his death in petting the dear little owls that had become so tame that they called to my sister and me whenever they saw us, and loved to have us take them in our hands and caress them.

About them I had no misgivings. They would certainly have died if I had not adopted them, and there was no question about their happiness. They were satisfied with a state of captivity. They had so far lost one of their owl habits, for they kept awake nearly all day, and slept nearly all night—and they could see quite well in the most brilliant Californian sunlight, and that is pretty brilliant. A cat or a dog many yards distant would cause them to raise excitedly the queer little ear tufts that play so prominent a part in the facial expression of some owls, and they would crack their beaks together and hiss angrily if the enemy came too near.

Cats and dogs frightened them, and a broom merely excited them. When strangers wanted to see the elevation of these tufts, a broom, swiftly passed over the floor, would cause Solomon and Betsy to become very wide awake, with feather tufts straight up in the air. I never saw them abjectly and horribly frightened but once. A lady had brought her handsome parrot into the room where the owls were. The poor little mites put up their ear tufts, swayed to and fro on their perch, and instead of packing their feathers and becoming thin and elongated in appearance, as they did for cats and dogs, they puffed themselves out, snapped their beaks, and uttered the loudest hissing noise I had ever heard from them.

From their extremity of fear I concluded that their instinct told them this danger was so imminent that they must make themselves as formidable as possible.

The parrot was of course quickly removed, and I took care that they should never again see another one.

CHAPTER II

THE OWLS START ON THEIR TRAVELS

Betsy and Solomon lived happily through that winter and spring, and before summer came we had made up our minds to return to the East. What should we do with the owls? They would be a great deal of trouble to some one. They required an immense amount of petting, and a frequent supply of perfectly fresh meat. No matter how busy we were, one of us had to go to the butcher every other day.

We began to inquire among our friends who would like a nice, affectionate pair of owls? There seemed no great eagerness on the part of any one to take the pets we so much valued. Plans for their future worried me so much that at last I said to my sister, "We will take them East with us."

The owls, who were to take so long a journey, became objects of interest to our friends, and at a farewell tea given to us, a smartly dressed young man vowed that he must take leave of Solomon and Betsy. Calling for a broom, he slowly passed it to and fro over the carpet before them, while they sat looking at him with lifted ear tufts that betrayed great interest in his movements.

We trembled a little in view of our past moving experiences, but we were devoted to the little creatures and, when the time came, we cheerfully boarded the overland train at Oakland.

We had with us Betsy and Solomon in their large cage, and in a little cage a pair of strawberry finches, so called because their breasts are dotted like a strawberry. A friend had requested us to bring them East for her. We had also a dog— not Teddy, that had only been lent to us; but our own Irish setter Nita, one of the most lovable and interesting animals that I have ever owned.

The chipmunk was no longer with us. He had not seemed happy in the aviary—indeed, he lay down in it and threw me a cunning look, as if to say, "I will die if you don't let me out of this." So I gave him the freedom of the house. That pleased him, and for a few days he was very diligent in assisting us with our housekeeping by picking all the crumbs off the floors and eating them. Then he disappeared, and I hope was happy ever after among the superb oak trees of the university grounds close to us.

When we started for the East, the pets, of course, had to go into the baggage car, and I must say here for the benefit of those persons who wish to travel with animals and birds, that there is good accommodation for them on overland trains. Sometimes we bought tickets for them, sometimes they had to go in an express car, sometimes we tipped the baggagemasters, but the sums spent were not exorbitant, and we found everywhere provision made for pets. You cannot take them in your rooms in hotels, but there is a place for them somewhere, and they will be brought to you whenever you wish to see them, or to give them exercise. We were on several different railway lines, and visited eight different cities, and the dog and birds, upon arriving in eastern Canada, seemed none the worse for their trip.

However, I would not by any means encourage the transportation of animals. Indeed, my feelings on the subject, since I understand the horrors animals and birds endure while being whirled from one place to another, are rather too strong for utterance. I would only say that in a case like mine, where separation between an owner and pets would mean unhappiness, it is better for both to endure a few days or weeks of travel. Then the case of animals and birds traveling with some one who sees and encourages them every day is different from the case of unfortunate creatures sent off alone.

Our Nita was taken out of the car at every station where it was possible to exercise her, and one of us would run into restaurants along the route to obtain fresh meat for the owls. Their cage was closely covered, but whenever they heard us coming they hooted, and as no one seemed to guess what they were, they created a great deal of interest. My sister and I were amused one evening in Salt Lake City to see a man bending over the cage with an air of perplexity.

"They must be pollies," he said at last, and yet his face showed that he did not think those were parrot noises issuing from within.

I remember one evening on arriving in Albany, New York, causing slight consternation in the hotel by a demand for raw meat. We hastened to explain that we did not want it for ourselves, and finally obtained what we wished.

As soon as we arrived home in Halifax, Nova Scotia, the owls were put downstairs in a nice, dry basement. They soon found their way upstairs, where the whole family was prepared to welcome them on account of their pretty ways and their love for caresses.

Strange to say, they took a liking to my father, who did not notice them particularly, and a mischievous dislike to my mother, who was disposed to pet them. They used to fly on her head whenever they saw her. Their little claws were sharp and unpleasant to her scalp. We could not imagine why they selected her head unless it was that her gray hair attracted them. However, we had a French Acadian maid called Lizzie, whose hair was jet black, and they disliked her even more than they did my mother.

Lizzie, to get to her storeroom, had to cross the furnace-room where the owls usually were, and she soon began to complain bitterly of them.

"Dey watch me," she said indignantly, "dey fly on my head, dey scratch me, an' pull out my hairpins, an' make my head sore."

"Why don't you push them off, Lizzie?" I asked, "they are only tiny things."

"Dey won't go—dey hold on an' beat me," she replied, and soon the poor girl had to arm herself with a switch when she went near them.

Lizzie was a descendant of the veritable Acadians mentioned in Longfellow's "Evangeline," of whom there are several thousand in Nova Scotia. My mother was attached to her, and at last she said, "I will not have Lizzie worried. Bring the owls up in my bathroom."

There they seemed perfectly happy, sitting watching the sparrows from the window and teasing my long-suffering mother, who was obliged to give up using gas in this bathroom, for very often the owls put it out by flying at it.

One never heard them coming. I did not before this realize how noiseless the flight of an owl is. One did not dream they were near till there was a breath of air fanning one's cheek. After we gave up the gas, for fear they would burn themselves, we decided to use a candle. It was absolutely necessary to have an unshaded light, for they would perch on any globe shading a flame, and would burn their feet.

The candle was more fun for them than the gas, for it had a smaller flame, and was more easily extinguished, and usually on entering the room, away would go the light, and we would hear in the corner a laughing voice, saying "Too, who, who, who, who!"

The best joke of all for the owls was to put out the candle when one was taking a bath, and I must say I heard considerable grumbling from the family on the subject. It seemed impossible to shade the light from them, and to find one's self in the dark in the midst of a good splash, to have to emerge from the tub, dripping and cross, and search for matches, was certainly not calculated to add to one's affection for Solomon and Betsy. However, they were members of the family, and as George Eliot says, "The members of your family are like the nose on your face—you have got to put up with it, seeing you can't get rid of it."

Alas! the time soon came when we had to lament the death of one of our troublesome but beloved pets.

Betsy one day partook heartily of a raw fish head, and in spite of remedies applied, sickened rapidly and sank into a dying condition.

I was surprised to find what a hold the little thing had taken on my affection. When her soft, gray body became cold, I held her in my hand close to the fire and, with tears in my eyes, wished for a miracle to restore her to health.

She lay quietly until just before she died. Then she opened her eyes and I called to the other members of the family to come and see their strange expression. They became luminous and beautiful, and dilated in a peculiar way. We hear of the eyes of dying persons lighting up wonderfully, and this strange illumination of little Betsy's eyes reminded me of such cases.

Even after death she lay with those wide-open eyes, and feeling that I had lost a friend, I put down her little dead body. It was impossible for me to conceal my emotion, and my mother, who had quite forgotten Betsy's hostility to her, generously took the little feathered creature to a taxidermist.

I may say that Betsy was the first and last bird I shall ever have stuffed. I dare say the man did the work as well as it could be done, but I gazed in dismay at my Betsy when she came home. That stiff little creature sitting on a stick, with glazed eyes and motionless body, could not be the pretty little bird whose every motion was grace. Ever since the day of Betsy's death, I can feel no admiration for a dead bird. Indeed, I turn sometimes with a shudder from the agonized postures, the horrible eyes of birds in my sister women's hats—and yet I used to wear them myself. My present conviction shows what education will do. If you like and study live birds, you won't want to wear dead ones.

After Betsy's death Solomon seemed so lonely that I resolved to buy him a companion. I chose a robin, and bought him for two dollars from a woman who kept a small shop. A naturalist friend warned me that I would have trouble, but I said remonstratingly, "My owl is not like other owls. He has been brought up like a baby. He does not know that his ancestors killed little birds."

Alas! When my robin had got beautifully tame, when he would hop about after me, and put his pretty head on one side while I dug in the earth for worms for him, when he was apparently on the best of terms with Sollie, I came home one day to a dreadful discovery. Sollie was flying about with the robin's body firmly clutched in one claw. He had killed and partly eaten him. I caught him, took the robin away from him, and upbraided him severely.

"Too, who, who, who who," he said—apologetically, it seemed to me, "instinct was too strong for me. I got tired of playing with him, and thought I would see what he tasted like."

I could not say too much to him. What about the innocent lambs and calves, of which Sollie's owners had partaken?

I had a fine large place in the basement for keeping pets, with an earth floor, and a number of windows, and I did not propose to have Sollie murder all the birds I might acquire. So, one end of this room was wired off for him. He had a window in this cage overlooking the garden, and it was large enough for me to go in and walk about, while talking to him. He seemed happy enough there, and while gazing into the garden or watching the rabbits, guineapigs, and other pets in the large part of the room, often indulged in long, contented spells of cooing—not hooting.

In 1902 I was obliged to leave him for a six months' trip

to Europe. He was much petted by my sister, and I think spent most of his time upstairs with the family. When I returned home I brought, among other birds, a handsome Brazil cardinal. I stood admiring him as he stepped out of his traveling cage and flew around the aviary. Unfortunately, instead of choosing a perch, he flattened himself against the wire netting in Sollie's corner.

I was looking right at him and the owl, and I never saw anything but lightning equal the celerity of Sollie's flight, as he precipitated himself against the netting and caught at my cardinal's showy red crest. The cardinal screamed like a baby, and I ran to release him, marveling that the owl could so insinuate his little claws through the fine mesh of the wire. However, he could do it, and he gripped the struggling cardinal by the long, hair-like topknot, until I uncurled the wicked little claws. A bunch of red feathers fell to the ground, and the dismayed cardinal flew into a corner.

"Sollie," I said, going into his cage and taking him in my hand, "how could you be so cruel to that new bird?"

"Oh, coo, coo, coo, coo," he replied in a delightfully soft little voice, and gently resting his naughty little beak against my face. "You had better come upstairs," I said, "I am afraid to leave you down here with that poor cardinal. You will be catching him again."

He cooed once more. This just suited him, and he spent the rest of his life in regions above. I knew that he would probably not live as long in captivity as he would have done if his lot had been cast in the California foothills. His life was too unnatural. In their native state, owls eat their prey whole, and after a time disgorge pellets of bones, feathers, hairs, and scales, the remnants of food that cannot be digested.

My owls, on account of their upbringing, wanted their food cleaned for them. Betsy, one day, after much persuasion, swallowed a mouse to oblige me, but she was such a dismal picture as she sat for a long time with the tail hanging out of her beak that I never offered her another.

I tried to keep Solomon in condition by giving him, or forcing him to take, foreign substances, but my plan only worked for a time.

I always dreaded the inevitable, and one winter day in 1903 I looked sharply at him, as he called to me when I entered the house after being away for a few hours. "That bird is ill!" I said.

No other member of the family saw any change in him, but when one keeps birds and becomes familiar with the appearance of each one, they all have different facial and bodily expressions, and one becomes extremely susceptible to the slightest change. As I examined Sollie, my heart sank within me, and I began to inquire what he had been eating. He had partaken freely of boiled egg, meat, and charcoal. I gave him a dose of olive oil, and I must say that the best bird or beast to take medicine is an owl. Neither he nor Betsy ever objected in the least to opening their beaks and taking any sort of a dose I was minded to give them.

The oil did him no good, and I saw that he was doomed. I kept him beside me during the night, and at four o'clock in the morning he died. Just at the last he opened his eyes, and there was the same strange, luminous, beautiful appearance of the eye-ball that there had been when Betsy died. I have seen many birds die, but have never, except in the case of the owls, noticed this opening of the eyes, with the curious illumination.

We missed the little fellow immensely, for he often insinuated his pretty little cooing note in the midst of our family conversation. He knew each one of us, and would call out when we came near him, but a stranger he always received in silence, and with raised ear tufts.

We tried not to mourn foolishly for our pet. The reproach is often and justly brought against animal-lovers that they are over-sensitive—that they love not wisely, but too well. We suffer, and the lower creation suffers with us. We lie down and die, and so must they. The rational and really happy way is to struggle against this passion of tenderness for all suffering, created things, to endeavor to be wise and practical, and while doing everything in our power to alleviate all suffering and unhappiness, yet not to be weakened by it.

Little Solomon had a happy life, and an almost painless death. There was only one thing lacking. We would like to look forward to seeing him again. Perhaps we shall—who knows?

CHAPTER III

A REIGN OF ROBINS

Bob the First, at the head of my long list of robins, having been killed by my pet owl, I very soon bought another. This one was not so gentle nor so handsome as Bob the First, his wings and his tail having their ends sawed off by contact with the wires of too small a cage.

Fearing that he might be lonely in my aviary with only rabbits, guineapigs, pet rats, and pigeons for company, I bought another robin called Dick. The new bird was long, straight, sharp-eyed, and much smarter in his movements than Bob the Second who, of course, considering the condition of his wings and tail, could not fly, and was obliged to hop over the ground.

It was very amusing to see the two robins stare at each other. Both had probably been trapped young, for at that time the law against the keeping of wild birds in captivity was not enforced, and boys and men were perniciously active in their depredations among our beautiful wild beauties.

Bob the Second was very fond of stuffing himself, and he used to drive the pigeons from the most promising window ledges and partake freely of the food scattered about.

Poor Dick ran about the ground looking for worms, and not finding many, got desperate and flew up to the window ledge.

Bob lowered his head and flew at him with open bill. Dick snapped at him, hopped up to the food, and satisfied his hunger, Bob meanwhile standing at a little distance, a queer, pained thread of sound issuing from between his bill, "Peep, peep, peep!"

A robin is a most untidy bird while eating, and as often as

Dick scattered a morsel of food outside the dish, Bob would spring forward and pick it up with a reproving air, as if he were saying, "What an extravagant fellow you are!"

Whenever a new bird enters an aviary, he has to find his place—he is just like a new-comer in a community of human beings. Bob, being alone, was in the lead when Dick came. Dick, having the stronger bird mind, promptly dethroned him. They were very amusing birds. Indeed, I find something clownish and comical about all robins kept in captivity.

The wild bird seems to be more businesslike. The partly domesticated bird, having no anxiety about his food supply, indulges in all sorts of pranks. He is curious and fond of investigation, and runs swiftly at a new object, and as swiftly away from it, if it seems formidable to him.

The arrival of new birds in the aviary always greatly excited Bob, and he hopped about, chirping, strutting, raising his head feathers, and sometimes acting silly with his food, just like a foolish child trying to "show off" before strangers.

When I introduced a purple gallinule to him, Bob flew up into the air, and uttered a shriek of despair. He feared the gallinule, and hated the first Brazil cardinal I possessed, and was always sparring with him. One day I put a second cardinal into the aviary. Bob thought it was his old enemy, and ran full tilt at him. His face of ludicrous dismay as he discovered his mistake and turned away, was too much for me, and I burst out laughing at him. I don't think he minded being made fun of. He flirted his tail and hopped away.

At one time Bob made up his mind that he would not eat crushed hemp-seed unless I mixed it with bread and milk, and he would throw it all out of his dish unless I made it in the way he liked.

My robins have always been good-natured, and I never saw one of them hurt the smallest or feeblest bird, though they will sometimes pretend that they are going to do so.

When Bob took a sun-bath, any member of the family who happened to be near him would always be convulsed with laughter. He would stretch his legs far apart, stick out his ragged plumage, elevate his head feathers till he looked as if he had a bonnet on, and then half shut his eyes with the most ludicrous expression of robin bliss.

All birds look more or less absurd when taking sun-baths. They seem to have the power to make each feather stand out from its neighbor. I suppose this is done in order that the sun may get to every part of the skin.

His most amusing performance, however, took place when his first moulting time after he came was over. One by one his old, mutilated feathers dropped out, and finally new ones took their places. On a memorable day Bob discovered that he had a real tail with a white feather on each side of it, and a pair of good, serviceable wings. He gave a joyful cry, shook his tail as if he would uproot it, then spread his wings and lifted himself in the air. Hopping time was over. He was now a real bird, and he flew from one end of the aviary to the other with an unmistakable expression of robin ecstasy.

Most unfortunately, I had not a chance to study poor Dick's character as fully as Bob's, for I only had him a short time. Both he and Bob, instead of mounting to perches at night, would go to sleep on the windowsills, where I was afraid my pet rats would disturb them, as they ran about in their search for food. Therefore, I went into the aviary every evening, and lifted them up to a comfortable place for the night, near the hot-water pipes. I would not put robins in a warm place now. They are hardy birds, and if given a sufficient quantity of nourishing food do not need a warm sleeping-place. If we only had a better food supply I believe we would have many more wild birds with us in winter in the Northern States and Canada than we have now.

Late one evening I went into the aviary to put my robins

to bed. I could only find Bob—Dick was nowhere to be seen. My father and mother joined me in the search, and finally we found his poor, lifeless body near the entrance to the rats' underground nest. His head had been eaten—poor, intelligent Dick; and in gazing at him, and at the abundance of food in the aviary, the fate of the rats was sealed.

I fed my birds hard-boiled egg mashed with bread crumbs, crushed hemp-seed, scalded cornmeal, bread and milk, prepared mockingbird food, soaked ant eggs, all kinds of mush or "porridge," as we say in Canada, chopped beef, potato and gravy, vegetables cooked and raw, seeds and fruit, an almost incredible amount of green stuff, and many other things—and yet the rats had found it necessary to commit a murder.

Well, they must leave the aviary, and they did, and for a time Bob reigned alone. I did try to bring up a number of young robins given to me by children who rescued them from cats, or who found them on the ground unable to fly, but for a long time I had very hard luck with them.

Either the birds were diseased or I did not feed them properly. I have a fancy that I half starved them. Bird fanciers whom I consulted told me to be sure and not stuff my robins, for they were greedy birds. As long as I took their advice my young robins died. When I went to my canaries for advice I saw that the parents watched the tiny heads folded like flowers too heavy for their stalks, over the little warm bodies in the nests.

The instant a head was raised the mother or father put a mouthful of warm egg-food in it. The little ones got all they would eat—indeed, the father, with food dripping from his mouth, would coax his nestlings to take just one beakful more. I smiled broadly and began to give my robins all the worms they wanted, and then they lived.

The bringing up of young birds is intensely interesting. I found that one reason why early summer is the favorite time for nest-making is because one has the short nights then. Parents can feed their young quite late in the evening and be up by early daylight to fill the little crops again. Robins are birds that like to sit up late, and are always the last to go to bed in the aviary.

I solved the difficulty of rising at daylight to feed any young birds I was bringing up by giving them a stuffing at eleven o'clock at night. Then I did not have to rise till nearly eight.

This, of course, was for healthy birds. If I had a sick guineapig, rabbit, or bird, I never hesitated to get up many times during the night, for I have a theory that men and women who cannot or will not undertake the moral responsibility of bringing up children, should at least assist in the rearing of some created thing, if it is only a bird. Otherwise they become egotistical and absorbed in self.

CHAPTER IV

A NAUGHTY MOCKINGBIRD

Among the young robins I had given me was one that was found sitting helplessly under some trees.

"I think I will try my solitary Bob with this one," I said, and I took it to the aviary and put it on the ground.

The baby robin that had been reserved and sulky with me, wildly flapped his tiny wings when he saw Bob, and ran after him screaming for food.

Bob stopped short, wheeled round, searching for worms, and diligently stuffed the little fellow, who followed him as closely as his shadow.

I was delighted with the success of my experiment, but received a shock a little later on going into the basement to find the wet, bedraggled body of my poor baby robin in the pigeon's big bathtub. He must have fluttered in while following Bob, his foster parent, about, and the puzzled Bob did not know how to get him out.

As I picked up the body and held him in my hand, a workman who was busy about some repairs in the basement, said solemnly, "It's drowned!" There was no doubt about it. I had lost my little bird, and now there was nothing but the burial.

Another little robin soon took its place. This one I promptly gave to Bob, and met with a surprise. The young one fluttered its little wings, ran after Bob with appealing cries to which a deaf ear was turned. Why would he not feed it?

"You selfish bird," I said, and I fed the robin myself.

Bob said nothing, but looked wise, and in a short time my baby robin was in a dying condition, crying and fluttering his little wings to the last, as if he saw the loving mother bird approaching with her bill full of food.

Had Bob refused to feed it because it was diseased? I fancied he had, for I usually find that birds know a good deal more about each other than I know about them.

Bob certainly knew a good deal more about himself than I did, for he soon gave me another surprise. The basement aviary was just under my study and my father's. Above the studies was a roof-veranda, and beyond the veranda was a sun-room. The veranda and sun-room were wired in so that the birds could not get out, but as there was no access to them through the studies, a narrow well or elevator, as we called it, had been built at the back of the house.

The birds went up and down this elevator like flashes of color, and seemed to enjoy the fun. Some of them preferred to sleep above, some below.

Among those that liked the roof-veranda was my long-legged gallinule. I had built him a nice broad nest in a sheltered place, and one summer night, to my amazement, I saw Bob hanging about him and giving him such plain hints to vacate the nest that at last the gallinule, being a gentlemanly bird, stepped off it and allowed Bob to step on.

I could not imagine why Bob was doing this curious thing. He had never made a nest nor slept in a nest, and had always perched on a branch. However, I made a practice of not interfering with my birds any more than I could help and, promising the gallinule a new nest on the morrow, I left them.

The next morning Bob stepped off the nest with such an air of importance that I hurriedly approached and looked in it. There lay a fine big robin's egg, and convulsed with laughter, I ran to proclaim the news to the family, "Old Bob the Second is not a male robin; he is a female."

Everybody came and stared, and Bob was the center of attraction for some time to come. She laid two other eggs and sat on them, and they amounted to nothing, whereupon she deserted the gallinule's nest and built one for herself. She sat on this one about three weeks, then deserted it and the three blue eggs and built another. This too was unprofitable, and she built another nest, and another, and another, until late autumn put an end to her nestmaking.

During that and successive summers I got to dread the time of nestmaking. I used to think I gave her plenty of mud, but there was rarely enough. She built a large, strong nest on some flat foundation, or in the forked branches of the firs and spruces I had standing about the aviary and roof veranda. When the mud gave out she mixed porridge with earth and soaked strips of paper in the water dishes. She kept things in a great mess, flinging sods of earth about, also sticks, straws, and feathers. While building the foundation she was always very dirty. After every beakful of soft substance was stuck round the framework, she would settle down in the middle of it, press her breast hard against the edge, and wheel round and round to keep the shape.

The most of her nests were built in the basement, and it was very amusing to see her hurry up the elevator to the roof-veranda, dart about there, and stuff her bill full of straws and grass, then start downward with a train of nest-material floating behind her. The soft, flexible grass was for the lining of the nest—the receptacle for her three precious blue eggs.

I used to pity Bob in her solitary nestmaking, and sometimes she gazed wistfully at the Virginian and Brazil cardinals and acted as if she wished they would both help her. They both disliked her, and having mates of their own, chased her away every time she went near them.

Sometimes I teased her by going up to the nest and telling her that she might as well give up—her eggs would amount to nothing. She would fly into a rage and take my fingers in her bill and scold, and sometimes scream at me.

However, a companion was on his way to her. A year later I

had sent to me a fine mockingbird—"the bird of four hundred tongues," as the Mexicans call him. He was a beauty, and quite an acrobat, for he would go to the top of the elevator and turn over and over in the air, flirting wings and tail as if to show the pretty white feathers in them. Bob took quite a fancy to this new bird, whom I named Dan, and soon a peculiar, querulous, uncomfortable sort of affection sprang up between them.

Dan used to sing a most fantastic song to her that sounded like "Git bang, git bang, cheer up, cheer up, meow, meow, meow!" varying it by imitations of the songs of other birds in the aviary, and also by the squealing of the guineapigs.

One day he got behind me and mimicked a guineapig in distress so cleverly that I turned round to aid it, but found only Dan with his mocking, inscrutable eye fixed on me.

Writes a sweet singer:
List to that bird, his song, what poet pens it?
Brigand of birds, he's stolen every note.
Prince though of thieves—look how the rascal spends it—
Pours the whole forest from one tiny throat.

Dan's affection for Bob was somewhat fitful. He flew about with her sometimes, and sometimes he took no notice of her beyond lowering his head and giving a spiteful hiss when she went near him. However, he would not allow any bird to disturb her in her nestmaking, and once when she deserted a nest and began to build a new one, he sat on the deserted one until two ringdoves drove him away and took possession of it themselves.

It was not long before I discovered that Dan's beautiful skin covered one of the naughtiest bird hearts I had ever known. He was so clever though, about the mischief he performed, that I rarely found him out until it was too late to punish him for it.

I often used to shut him up in the owl's cage for punishment, and I felt convinced that he knew what he went in there for, as he was always better after coming out.

His wickedness consisted in persistent bullying. He was no fighter. His slender body and bill proclaimed that. His chief pleasure in life was to mischievously frighten birds from their food.

Sometimes he would select a bird as large as a pigeon. I have seen a big fantail spring from the ground in nervous terror when Dan, with a menacing hiss, came rushing at him from some sheltered nook.

His attacks were always in the rear, when it was a case of a large bird. If he had dared to attack the pigeon in front, the big fellow would have given him a disdainful peck.

One day I found a Java sparrow dead in a box beside her nest full of eggs. Poor little mother bird! Here was some tragedy. I picked up her emaciated body, and watched her mate.

He was thin and nervous in appearance, and taking advantage of my appearance in the aviary, was trying to pick up some of the white French millet seeds, of which he was very fond. He was meanwhile keeping a wary eye on Dan, who did not dare to attack him in my presence.

I read the whole story. The little mother had succumbed first, for the times of eating would be few and far between, compared with those of her mate. She had died for her nest—had sat on the eggs till her half-starved condition forced her to succumb. I gave Dan a wrathful glance and took the male Java to a sunny room upstairs, where he soon became as fat as a partridge.

CHAPTER V

A ROBIN AND SPARROW FRIENDSHIP

Another one of Dan's victims was a pine grosbeak, a most amiable, gentle bird that I rescued from a small cage in a bird-store.

My grosbeak was a greenish-gray bird, with a stout beak and intelligent eyes. More than any bird I had ever had, did her expression remind me of that on the face of a human being. I scarcely looked at her without thinking of a friend—a handsome woman with a well-developed nose. I never had a gentler, kinder bird, nor one that became tame in so short a time. She loved human society, and would follow any of the family about, perching on our heads or shoulders and taking seeds from our lips. Indeed, she soon became so tame that she would take food from the hands of utter strangers.

One pretty trick she had was to go sailing on the blocks of wood that I put in the big water dishes for the little birds to light on. The grosbeak took the greatest delight in perching on these blocks and floating from one side of a dish to the other.

I knew that the mockingbird did not like her, but she was so large—about eight inches long, and had such a stout beak that I knew he could not hurt her, and I hoped she would get over her dread of him. She did not. He frightened her, and made her feel so timid in the basement that she took to sleeping in the elevator. Then she began to come up on the veranda, and if the gate leading to it were closed she would stand beside it and tap on the wire till I let her in.

At last I took her upstairs, and there she had a happy winter, though she never seemed very strong. One day I was amused to see her sitting beside my sister, who was cracking sunflower seeds for her—the grosbeak being either too lazy or too miserable that day to do it for herself. My sister would open the seed and give the grosbeak the contents. The grosbeak watched her intently, and if ever so small a piece fell on the floor she would fly down and pick it up.

As a family, the grosbeaks are very trustful birds, and are said to stare at a hunter approaching them with a gun, and will continue to stare, even after he has shot down one or more. They are extremely affectionate with each other, and one grosbeak has been known to follow its mate into captivity.

However, they are not foolish birds, judging from the one I had. She was sweet and trusting, but also intelligent. When the early summer came she died, to the very great regret of the whole family, and I always blamed Dan for undermining her constitution by his bullying.

I had, however, become foolishly fond of this bird, and could not bear to part with him, and kept him in my aviary until this autumn, when I made up my mind that he was really too bad to be left at home without my supervision.

I sent him to an aviary where he would have more room than with me, and would be with larger birds. When the first reports came from him, one of the family remarked that handsome Dan always fell on his feet. He was getting special care and attention, but—and I could not help smiling—one bird had singled him out for persecution, as he had so often singled out weaker ones for persecution in his day. Dan's enemy was an English blackbird, who was pursuing him so relentlessly that one of her flight feathers had to be pulled out so that she could not catch up to him. I hope this affliction may make him a better bird, and may cause him to reflect that there is a great law of retribution in the bird as well as in the human world.

To return to the robins—Bob went on with her nestmaking, and soon I had another robin brought to me who grew up to look so much like her that she was a veritable Bob the Third. This baby robin was about the best one I ever brought up. It was the same old story—fallen from the nest, no parents near, and cats abounding, so I adopted the little Bobbie, carried her about on my finger, and as the house was full of company took her every night in one hand, and her dish of worms in the other, downstairs in my father's study to sleep on a big sofa bed.

The walls were lined with books, and pulling out one from its fellows I would put Bobbie on it. There she sat all night, but when daylight came she began to chirp politely and remind me that a hungry robin was near. This bird was never one bit of trouble. At one time I left her to go to the country to buy a farm. She took her food from my sister, and later on, when I moved all my birds to the farmhouse, she settled down in her rooms there, as if she had always been accustomed to them.

I kept her a year, then opening the door, told her to fly outside if she wished. She did wish, and calmly went to the flower garden, hopped about there for a while, followed the men plowing near-by, then accepting the advances made to her by a respectable-looking wild robin, built a nest on one of the house windows, raised a family of young robins, and I hope, went south with them when autumn came, for I have seen nothing of her since.

My next robin was my beloved Dixie, and I have had him only a few months. During June of the year 1907 I saw, on looking out of the windows of the little sun-room on the top of the house, that a pair of robins had built a nest at the back of the box on a tall telephone post near-by. They seemed to have young ones on one side of it, and a pair of sparrows seemed to have their young ones on the other side.

I kept watch, and soon I saw the old robins going in and out with worms hanging from their beaks. At night the mother robin would sit on the nest, and the father would perch in a tall tree across the street. He might have sat close to her, if our beautiful big elms in front of the house had not been killed by some mysterious disease.

One June day, as I sat writing in my study, I heard a pair of birds having hysterics in our garden, and springing up, I went to the window. They were robins of course—it seems to me that of all the birds I know, the robin is the most noisy and fussy when danger threatens him. Instead of keeping still, which might have enabled them to have their little nestling with them, they were yelling at the tops of their voices because he had flown into the garden and could not get out. Therefore, at their outcry, a ring of little faces surrounded the fluttering baby.

"Please go away, children," I called out, and they obediently disappeared.

"Now," I reflected, "if I can only keep the cats off!"

By some miracle, the cats did not enter our garden that morning, but I was sorry to see that the little robin could not rise higher than the fence. The parents were too frightened to feed him there, and at last I went out and tried to catch him.

In vain—I, of course, was as formidable to him as a cat, and when he saw me coming he managed to flutter over the fence into the street, and to the low branch of a tree. I promptly returned to the house, and in a few minutes he was in the garden again. I tried not to watch him. The cats would soon get him—and what was one robin more or less, anyway?

It was a good deal—it was the whole world to me that morning, and any bird-lover will understand my feelings. I would write a little, then would hurry to the window to see that no enemy came near that precious baby bird. I admired his calmness. He sat all the morning on a fence-post, and only toward noon did he slip under some raspberry bushes. I hoped that his parents might find him there, but I doubted it, and with a sinking heart I went away to fulfil an engagement.

I could not keep the stoical little birdie out of my thoughts, and the sequel to his story is as strange as a made-up one.

At dusk I returned home, and on going upstairs was surprised to hear a loud robin-chirp near me. I followed the sound, and there, sitting in the middle of the upstairs bathroom floor, stoical no longer, but clamorous, now that no cats were near, was my robin baby of the morning.

"You blessed thing!" I exclaimed, catching him up. "However did you get in here?"

I looked at the window. It was screened, as were all the windows in the house, to keep the birds in, and the cats out. The little fellow, when night came on, had been warned by his instinct to get up high. He had flown or scrambled up the side of the house, perhaps by means of an ash tree trained against the wall, and had gone up the screen, and then down, where it did not quite fit against the sash.

I had never had a bird perform such a feat, and I said soberly to him, "Providence has delivered you into my hands."

He looked distrustfully at me. He did not care much for me in those days, but in his hunger he soon forgot his shyness. His poor little crop was quite empty. I fed him all he would eat, and in a few days he had forgotten his parents, and fluttered his little wings, and called for food whenever he saw me coming.

I called him Dixie, and put him in a cage with a young sparrow that a boy had brought me a few days before, saying that a painter had sent it. The man had been at work on a house, and this young one had fallen out of its nest. He was so young that he soon forgot his parents, and, like the robin, shook his wings when he saw me coming, and called for food.

Amusing to relate, the little sparrow took a violent fancy to the robin, and looking upon him as a second parent, followed him all about the cage begging for food. The young robin was dreadfully embarrassed. He could not feed himself—how could he feed another bird? Sometimes when the sparrow's pursuit grew too hot, he would stop running, and turning, would face the smaller bird with wide-open bill, as if to say, "Look for yourself—there is no food in there."

The sparrow was not to be reasoned with. He never stopped his pursuit of the robin, except to rest. At first I permitted it, for it gave them both exercise. Then, when the exercise increased till it became over-exertion, I took them both out of the cage and put them on the roof-veranda. By this time the sparrow could feed himself, but the robin could not. With strange inconsistency, the smaller bird would stuff himself with bread and milk, or egg-food, then he would run after the robin with his cry of, "More, more!"

The poor robin would run from one side of the veranda to the other, skipping over food and water dishes, and occasionally stopping short, and turning on the sparrow with wide-open bill.

The sparrow never gave up the chase until Dixie eluded him by slipping into some hiding-place. Then he would go all about, peering into corners with his sharp little eyes till he found him.

I have heard strangers utter shrieks of laughter at this peculiar pursuit of the robin by the sparrow. When these two birds grew older it was just as amusing, for then they flew from place to place.

CHAPTER VI

DIXIE AND TARDY

When Dixie was about three weeks old he became afflicted by a cough. He had a mania for bathing. I could not keep him out of the water dishes. He was soaked from morning till night, and finally he sounded like a consumptive robin. I tried shutting him in a cage, but that fretted him; and when he came out he was more anxious to bathe than ever. The cough hung about him for weeks, and I made up my mind that I was going to lose him, but he finally recovered from it.

I used to hear him coughing at night, for I slept in a room opening off the roof-veranda. I would put my head out the doorway in the morning, and say, "Well, Dixie, how is the cough?" He knew quite well that I was addressing him, and would give a little croupy bark in answer. I became so fond of him, and his cough clung to him so late in the season, that I resolved to keep him. Not so with the sparrow. I thought it would be better to let him go, and one day I put him outside the wire netting.

I never saw a more surprised bird. He had forgotten the nest on the side of the house, the tiny, sooty parent-birds. The robin was his father, his mother, his world. He ran to and fro over the wire netting, he looked down at his friend, at the nice food and the fresh seeds, and his regret was so keen, that I said consolingly, "If you keep that up, little fellow, I will let you come back again."

I always keep a certain amount of food outside the aviary for street sparrows and pigeons, so the little exile did not suffer, and in time he forgot the robin, and only occasionally visited him.

Dixie grew and flourished, and is now a very fine-looking

bird. A few weeks ago he began to practise some fine rolling notes that promise a fine singer. He stopped singing when I put him into the warm basement for the winter. He was very indignant, and shook his tail as he talked to me about taking him off the roof-veranda.

I remonstrated with him, and told him of his weak throat, and that I wished him to get perfectly strong during the winter, so that next spring he might fly away with the wild birds if he wished to do so. He looked as if he understood. He is a very intelligent bird, and when he wishes to dig worms that are beneath his reach, he lets me know it.

I found this out one evening, when I had forgotten to go at dusk and dig him his final supper. I had taken a book, and was lying on a sofa in the veranda-room, when I was aware that a very disconsolate little figure was staring at me through the glass.

"What is the matter, Dixie?" I asked.

He at once flew to his box of worms, and taking the hint, I went out and dug some.

I must put the digging of worms in the past tense. Dixie has lately refused to eat them. That happens with every robin I have possessed. Old Bob gave up eating worms long ago. Robins seem to like egg-food, bread and milk, meat, and almost any kind of civilized food better than angleworms. They will all eat mealworms—the fat, yellowish worms that are raised especially for birds, but the plebeian earthworms they soon tire of. Evidently they do not require them, for Bob is in excellent condition, making seven and eight nests a summer, and being, I do not know how many years old. I have had her for nearly seven.

Last, and best loved of my robins, because I snatched him from the jaws of death, is Tardy—so named because he was a late autumn baby, being brought to me on the fifth of September. He was plump and well-favored when he came, but

I made the same mistake with him that I made with Dixie—I let him bathe too early.

It is a most amusing thing to see a robin with his first bath. He is never surprised at worms. They come as a matter of course. But put a dish of water in his cage. He has never had water before, except from a medicine-dropper. He stares at this little bathtub. What is that glittering in it?

He springs forward to investigate, runs backward in fear of the gleaming, shimmering liquid. What can it be! He plucks up courage, and bravely strikes the edge of the dish. It does not strike back. He becomes bolder, and dabs his beak in the center. What is this flying into his eyes? He chokes, coughs, gets a drop of the liquid down his throat, tastes, swallows, and runs at it again.

"Hooray!" he chirps in robin joy. "It is fine! I'll get into it," and down he goes, and the happy beholder of a robin's first bath has hard work to suppress a peal of laughter.

No boy with his first pants, first pony, or first anything, can excel the joy of a young robin with his first bath—and like a too-indulgent parent, I made the same mistake with Tardy that I did with Dixie, and let him have as many as he liked.

It seemed incredible to me that wild birds could or would bathe too much. Yet they do, and too late I shut Tardy up and took his bath away. The mischief had been done, and I suppose my little bird really had something like pneumonia.

I was quite upset about his illness, and made up my mind that he should not die, if I could make him live. I have nursed many birds and animals, had many a stubborn fight with their king of terrors, but I never had such hard work to keep breath in a little bird's body as I had with Tardy.

He became hollow-chested and emaciated, the feathers came out of his head. He was bald while yet a baby, his long legs made him look as if he were on stilts, he coughed persistently, he became snappish and peevish, and sometimes refused to eat.

Night after night I got up every few hours, and coaxed him to take something, for he was like a weak patient that would die if left too long without nourishment.

"I won't," he would snap angrily, as I offered him a worm at two p. m.

"Oh, please," I would coax him. "Good Tardy!"

"Well, just to oblige you," he would seem to say at last, and the worm would go down.

"Now another, Tardy boy."

"I will not," and this tone was final.

Then I had to open his beak, and he would cough and nearly choke, and I would feel that I was killing him, and would glance toward the chloroform bottle that I kept standing near him, for I was resolved not to let him suffer too much.

I never chloroform an animal or bird that has a chance to get well, even if it undergoes some suffering in the process. Often, as I sit by some intelligent, suffering creature, I try to express to it in some way the hope that it will have courage to endure bravely—just as one says to a human being, "Bear up—be courageous—your pain will soon be over."

When one speaks in this way, it is touching to see how responsive are the members of the lower creation. Naturally, if their sufferings are too great, they are, like us, utterly oblivious of what goes on around them. But, if there is only intermittent pain, they seem to appreciate one's sympathy.

Tardy's illness made him very intelligent and very dependent on me, but the time came when I thought he ought to feed himself.

I can always tell by the length of a young robin's tail when he is old enough to look after his own food supply, but Tardy's tail grew until it was almost as long as an old bird's, yet he would not eat a morsel himself. He would fly at me on the rare occasions when he wanted food, would scream, peck at me, and go to his dish of worms.

I would take a spoon, lift a worm, and say, "There it is, pick it up for yourself."

He would put his head on one side, and stare at it, knowing quite well what I meant, but would not touch it.

Then I would relent and hand it to him, and if it was neither too long nor too short, nor too fat nor too lean, he would take it.

He was, as indeed most robins are, a very extravagant bird, and would eat some worms and throw the rest about.

Sometimes I had hard work to find boys to dig worms for me, but no matter how busy or how tired I was, the supply must be kept up, for while he was young he liked nothing else.

He was a very nervous bird, and I never caught him sleeping, no matter how quietly I stole into the room. This was unnatural. A young bird should not do much else but sleep and eat. To my great joy, the cough, after a time, began to leave him, and he condescended occasionally to feed himself.

When I found I was obliged to leave home I did considerable worrying about my sick robin. However, a kind maid that I had had on my farm promised to take the best of care of him, and after laying in a stock of worms, and engaging a boy to bring more, I came away.

This maid writes me constantly about all my birds. Of Tardy she remarks, "The Robin in the Chage is a verry dirty Bird. I can't keep him clean, and if I give him a paper in his Chage he will tear it up. He eats Lamb now and Ant eggs. The Feathers are growing on his Head."

After hearing this, I wrote her to put him in the aviary, where I hope he will make friends with Bob and Dixie, and spend a happy winter.

My only regret is, that during my absence, my little bird

will lose his pretty, affectionate ways. He will never again call to me, nor take my fingers in his beak and play with them. Nor will he strike me—but perhaps it is just as well that he should take his rightful place, as a plain, unaccomplished robin.

The Tardy who was afraid of all other birds, who was so nervous that he would not eat if I took a stranger in his room, was not in his proper sphere. The new Tardy will, I hope, be a strong bird, able to fly away with his fellows when the lovely springtime comes.

I used to have a great liking for, and approval of, accomplished pets in the lower creation. Now, unless in exceptional circumstances, I would rather see an animal or a bird live his own life in the sphere in which God has placed him.

The trained birds and animals that used to give me so much pleasure are now distressing sights to me. Why should little canaries be taught to wear jackets, and fire cannon, and draw little carts? They don't like it—they can't like it. Those actions are contrary to bird nature. They were created birds. Why not let them be birds? Bird intelligence is not human intelligence, and it seems foolish to try and wrest it into a semblance of ours.

I now let my pets do just exactly what they wish to do in the line of accomplishments. I always carry on a certain amount of supervision and discipline in the way of not allowing them to injure each other, but they do no tricks, unless they fall into them naturally.

It used to be a great pleasure to us as a family to teach our dogs tricks. Now we allow them to be plain dogs, unless they pick up certain intelligent ways. The sight of trained dogs is now almost a revolting one to me. No one can persuade me that dogs like to do the unnatural things required of them.

CHAPTER VII

RABBITS AND GUINEAPIGS

One of the first inhabitants of my aviary in Halifax was a spotted rabbit.

I had always been fond of rabbits. My parents had kept them for my brothers when we were children, and during my stay in California I had had a pet pair that I obtained one day in an absent-minded way.

I was going shopping in Berkeley, and my sister said, "We need a coffeepot. I wish you would bring one home." When I returned she asked for the coffeepot, and I was obliged to confess that I had forgotten it, but I had bought a fine pair of rabbits instead.

These two became great pets, and used to play about the yard with my gentle dog, Nita, but I had to give them away when I left Berkeley. On reaching Halifax, I at once got this little spotted animal, and subsequently bought a pretty gray one to bear him company.

My poor spotted rabbit did not live long. One of our fox-terriers, Jim by name, a young, enthusiastic romp, played so hard with him that he injured him. I put the unfortunate little creature in a box where he lay turning from side to side for a day, and then, in spite of brandy and oil administered in small doses, he died.

I have never yet found that brandy helped a sick bird or animal. Warm milk and oil are now my stimulants—that is, for simple ailments. For complicated cases, I consult our family physician, who is most kind in prescribing for my pets.

The boy from whom I bought the spotted rabbit said that a sick rabbit is a dead rabbit. I disproved this later, but by the death of this spotted one I painfully added to my stock of knowledge, and I resolved that never again would I allow a rabbit to play with a puppy as rough as the lively Jim.

After the death of Spotty, Rab, the gray one, seemed lonely with only birds for companions, so I decided I would get her some guineapigs to play with, and accordingly ransacked the city for them.

I could find none, but one day two little girls came to our door and asked for me. "Would you—would you," they said in choked voices, "take our dear little guineapig? We know you want one, and we think ours would have a better home with you than with us."

"My dear children," I replied, "I could not think of taking your guineapig from you. Why, you are almost crying at the thought of parting from it."

"Oh! we want you to have it," they said, "but please don't think we want to get rid of her. We just love her, but we know you will love her better, and it is our duty to do what is best for her, and not to think of our own pleasure."

Charmed with these children, whose grandfather I found had been a Canadian naturalist, who had built aviaries and houses for birds and animals in his park, I said, "Well, you may bring Guinea to me, but only as a loan. I will give her back to you in the spring."

The little girls thanked me heartily, and said, "Now she will not be lonely. We have to keep her in our basement when we are away at school, and sometimes we think she is cold."

I told them that our basement contained plenty of hot-water pipes, and that I hoped the rabbit would be a good friend to their Piggy.

They went away, and some days later, when I was not at home, they arrived with the pig in a basket.

Lizzie doubtfully took the basket up to my mother, who

was in bed.

"A peeg for Miss Marshall."

My long-suffering mother, accustomed to a great variety of pets in times past, had never yet had a pig foisted upon her, though she had put up with a snake.

"A pig!" she exclaimed, "in that basket! It must be a young one. Put your hand in, Lizzie."

Lizzie, though usually demure and obedient, flatly refused, whereupon my mother said, "Perhaps there is some mistake. If my daughter intended to have a pig, she would have got a larger one than this. Tell the little girls they may leave it, if they like, but perhaps it would be safer to call again with it."

The little girls refused most decidedly to leave the pig, and when I came home I felt badly, knowing that they must have been disappointed.

The next day I hastened to their house, and their mother told me some interesting stories with regard to her children's fondness for pets.

On one occasion they had taken this same little guineapig to the country, and had one afternoon gone four miles from home. Rather than spend the night away from their little pet, they walked back the four miles to get to her.

I waited until they arrived from school, and seeing me, they ran to get Piggy, who was a pretty, broken-colored, short-haired English pig that had been brought to them from the West Indies.

With some trepidation I saw this precious pig put into a basket and entrusted to my care. On arriving home I carried her to the aviary, where my solitary rabbit was rambling alone, and put her on the ground.

Happy little Guinea—she had lived so long away from other animals that she fell into an ecstasy on seeing Rab, and with grunts and squeals of delight ran about the aviary just as fast as her short legs would carry her.

Rab stopped short, stared at the demonstrative stranger, then, to my mingled amusement and dismay, gave her a decided kick.

The unfortunate Guinea drew back. Such a hint was not to be misunderstood. However, she continued to follow and admire the unfeeling Rab at a distance, Rab, meanwhile, pretending neither to see her nor to hear her. I pitied Guinea so much that I began to ransack the city for other guineapigs.

One day a boy told me to go to Grafton Street, and in a house there I found a woman with a family of children.

I asked them whether they had guineapigs.

They said yes, they had some nice white prize pigs, and they would be glad to part from some of them, for the winter was coming on, and hungry rats had already devoured several of the little ones.

One of the boys ran out and brought in three little pigs, very unlike my dark Guinea, for these were white, with long hair all blown the wrong way, as if they had been out in a gale of wind. "Abyssinian," I believe is the name of this kind of pig. The Peruvians have still longer hair.

It seems that guineapigs have nothing to do with Guinea, and are not pigs at all. They are derived from the wild cavy, and were domesticated by the Mexicans of Peru. The Dutch introduced them into Europe during the sixteenth century, where they became great pets with children on account of their gentleness and pretty ways.

My mother, upon my arriving home with three more pigs, was astonished but resigned, and soon they became her special pets. I had now four, and my Guinea was in pig raptures that sent all the family into fits of laughter. Like a train of little cars, they ran along the path and up the bank, and over the bank, and down again on the earth floor of the aviary. Their little bodies were elongated, their feet were barely visible, and at frequent intervals they raised their heads, and uttered queer, piercing squeals of delight. Sometimes they made a curious continued sound like the running of a sewing-machine. The squeals came in moments of excitement, particularly when it was mealtime.

They liked bread and milk, hay, oats, and corn, and all kinds of vegetables. They also drank water. My rabbits too have liked water, and my experience with animals and birds has taught me always to keep fresh water before them. If they don't like it, they won't drink it.

I have heard some persons say that guineapigs are stupid. I never found mine stupid. I never saw an animal suffer more from homesickness than one of these Abyssinian guineapigs called Tiny. Later on, I had more rabbits, and one day I took Tiny from the aviary and put her in the furnace-room to bear company to a sick rabbit. This little white rabbit affectionately licked his guineapig friend, but Tiny was so ill, and so frightened with him, that I took compassion on her, and put her back with her companions.

She was so supremely happy to get back, and so excited that she could not eat, and when a guineapig or any other kind of a pig cannot eat, it is very deeply moved. Scampering to and fro over the earth, she smelled food-dishes, boxes, and the barrel laid on its side that was her bedroom. That showed her love of locality. Then she saluted her little friends with nose-touchings and piggy yells of bliss, and finally fell soberly to munching hay.

I suppose one should strive against the tendency to humanize birds and animals, yet one cannot help admiring and sympathizing when one finds them showing like qualities with ourselves. Take this capacity for homesickness, for example. Apart from the torture of captivity, experienced by a wild bird when caged even in a large place, there is a dislike on the part of birds and animals that are reconciled to a state of captivity to being moved from one place to another. Some time ago I was visiting an aviary, and while waiting for the curator had some conversation with a pair of cockatoos that were walking in and out of his office, apparently very much at home. One of them started to gnaw the scrap basket to pieces, and when I advised him to desist, lest his master should be angry with him, he gave me a peculiarly intelligent glance, and walked out of the room.

When the curator arrived, he told me the birds were suffering from homesickness. Wishing to have some repairs made in their large cage, he had moved them to another, where they pined visibly, and at last became ill. Being great pets, he was keeping them with him; and after a time, I was pleased to hear, they both recovered.

To return to the guineapigs—to those persons who insist on saying they are stupid, I would like to state that I never saw any animal or any bird kinder to the young of other animals or birds than those same guineapigs.

I have seen human mothers kind and devoted to their own children, and to say the least of it, neglectful and egotistical when it came to the offspring of others. I have seen dogs, cats, and birds absolutely hateful to the young of their own kind. I never saw, even an old grandfather guineapig, in any way intentionally injure or molest a baby guineapig, or any other kind of a baby. I have seen them go round them or over them, but never bite, or push, or snarl, or snap at young ones. Occasionally, I have known old pigs to kill young ones accidentally, on account of their love of sociability.

They all slept in barrels with plenty of newspapers and straw to keep the young ones warm, and as they were very fond of calling on each other, particularly when there was the excitement of twins or triplets in a family, they would sometimes crowd too closely in a barrel, and smother a baby to death.

CHAPTER VIII

MY PET RATS

I was very much interested in these baby guineapigs, and was very much surprised to find them so fully developed at birth. Tiny and Guinea had families about the same time, and I found all the little pigs with pretty, soft-haired bodies, open eyes, and their teeth through, the milk teeth being already shed. In a few hours they could run by the side of their mothers, and in two days they could nibble vegetables.

Unfortunately, Guinea became ill, also her brown baby. I gave her white baby to Tiny, who was an excellent foster-mother to it, and taking Guinea and Brownie upstairs, I put them on a hot-water bag.

In watching Guinea I shuddered, thinking of the grief of the little girls, should she die. She breathed rapidly all the afternoon and evening. If I had dosed her with castor or sweet oil, it might have done good, but I did not think of it. At midnight she jumped up, ran around the room, gasped for breath, and died. I put her in a white box and sent for her little owners, who came sadly to see her. Never would I have believed it possible that one could become so much attached to a guineapig.

Guinea's young one did well in the basement; the brown one died after I had fussed over it for a week, getting up two or three times at night, and stretching out my hand to poor Brownie, who would crawl on it to be fed.

I had the over-zeal of ignorance, and gave poor Piggy undiluted cow's milk. Common sense might have taught me that a little water and a little sugar should be added to the milk of a great strong creature like a cow, when fed to any small animal. Afterward, I brought up several young guineapigs whose parents had died. Just at first one has to use a medicine-dropper or teaspoon to feed them, but in a marvelously short time they will stick their own little noses in their bread and milk.

One of my favorite pigs was a dark-colored, long-haired Peruvian, that looked like a weeping willow, minus its trunk.

When I first got him his funereal appearance seriously affected some of my birds. He lived, and was happy with me, and when I moved my pets to my farm I took him and the other pigs with me. They so much enjoyed the delicious red and white clover, and the kind attention of a relative to whom I gave them, that when I sold my farm, I left my pigs behind me. However, I have quite missed them, and often think that some day I must again start a nursery of guineapigs.

I became very much fonder of them than of my rabbits. They were very much better behaved, though I must acknowledge, that as far as my experience with children goes, rabbits seem to have more power than the gentle pigs of inspiring a warm affection.

The most enthusiastic rabbit-lovers I have ever known were two little girls, who came to me one day with a pair of tiny white rabbits. Would I give these little creatures a home? I was very glad to do so, for I thought that my gray Rab, who was now a big handsome rabbit, would not despise these creatures of her own kind, as she had despised the guineapig. I put the little white fellows in with her, and to my surprise she darted at them, and tried to injure them in such an unmistakable way that I promptly pounced on her and took her out in the furnace-room. She did not like this, and gazed angrily through the wire door at the white rabbits that were careering around with the guineapigs. She had been naughty, but still I was sorry for her. On remembering her first friend, the spotted rabbit, I bought another to play with her. She got on very well with this new friend, but the little white rabbits fell into misfortune.

On going into the aviary one morning, I found one of them cold in death. What had happened to him? There was nothing there that could injure him. After some hard thinking and Sherlock Holmes examination of tracks and signs, I discovered that during the night the poor little rabbit had started to eat hay on the edge of the long, steep bank of earth, had fallen down, and could not find the path leading to his little brother above. He had died of fright, and I soon had the bank low enough for guineapigs and rabbits to run up and down. The surviving rabbit became ill, so I put him out in the warmer furnace-room, and drove Rab and Spotty to the aviary.

This made fresh trouble. Rab had been quite upset when I took her from the aviary, and now she was more upset because I had put her back. She had become accustomed to the furnace-room, and she shook the wire door, and gnawed the woodwork, and at last, seeing the rage she was in, I allowed her to return to the furnace-room. She was so ill that she lay down as if she were going to die. I slipped a hot-water bag under her, and advised her to keep on it. She gazed about her in a peculiar way with laid-back ears, looking as if she did not think much of my opinion. However, she kept on the bag, only occasionally getting up to take a long drink of cold water, and in a day or two was quite well.

While she was ill she did not molest the rabbit, nor did her companion, Spotty, interfere with him. He was a pretty good rabbit, and not bad-tempered, as Rab was. As soon as she recovered she sought the young rabbit's life, and I was obliged to have a stout enclosure made for him, as I still wished to keep him in the warm furnace-room. I knew there were rats in this room. We saw them running about with Rab and Spotty, eating their grain with them, drinking from their water dishes, nestling in their bundle of hay, and sitting by the furnace to keep warm. I have always had a liking for rats, and it did not occur to me that these well-fed creatures, with the peculiarly bright, intelligent eyes, could or would kill my baby rabbit.

However, they did do so; and one January afternoon when I went to the basement to feed my downstairs family, I was shocked to discover his little blood-stained body in my path. The cruel rats had entered the wire pen of the little fellow, had dragged out his body, and had eaten his brains.

I ran for my father, who was always most sympathetic. He said he did not see how the rats had pried up the heavy supports of the rabbit's cage. However, they had done it; and I wrapped poor Bunny up and put him in the furnace—cremation being my preferred mode of disposing of my pets' bodies.

Then we spent the evening in making a trap for the rats, but I fancy they watched us while we were doing it, and we, of course, caught none of them. We did catch some young ones, however, and the five tiny things looked so innocent as they sat in their trap that I could not make up my mind to have them killed, and took the cage up to my father's study.

"Suppose we keep them," I suggested, "and train them— make them friendly with the young rabbits and pigs and birds."

"Suppose we do," he said; and leaving his books, he descended to the aviary with me, and together we rigged a big cage against one of the brick walls. There the rat babies could look at my pets, and get acquainted with them.

Young rats are really pretty creatures. These little ones had white breasts, pink paws, shell-like, whitish ears, black whiskers, and bright, black eyes. They slept all day in a brown box at the top of their big cage. This box looked something like a pulpit, and, if roused, they would lean over their pulpit, holding on by their pink paws, their beady eyes seeming to say, "What do you want? We don't like to play till night comes."

One day one of them became ill, and lay under the straw at the bottom of the cage for some time. It was almost human to see the way in which he would stretch one little pink paw from under the straw, and feebly move it to and fro.

When these young rats were partly grown, we caught two tiny ones and put in with them. The new-comers were very anxious to get up in the brown box, and tried climbing up hand over hand, or rather paw over paw toward it. The big ones amused themselves by leaning out of the box and pushing them down. I gave the little ones a tangle of wool to sleep in on the bottom of the cage, and two or three days later the older ones relented, and allowed them to climb up to sleep in the box.

It seemed to me particularly appropriate that my father, who is a doctor of divinity, should take an interest in the training of these young rats. So I was amused when he proposed to give them a whirligig. This wheel was put in the cage, and soon my father had his rat students so trained that when he struck the cage sharply, and said, "Come, boys!" one of them would spring from the pulpit, his little feet flying, his black eyes excited, and his whole appearance apparently denoting his appreciation of the amusement of his spectators in his mechanical performance, though I finally concluded that the intelligent creature was supremely bored by it.

After a time one of these young rats managed in some way or other to squeeze himself out of the cage. I did not concern myself greatly about it. I intended to give every one of them their freedom some day, but I was sorry for his evident loneliness, and amused beyond description to see him one day trying to insinuate himself back into the cage.

He spent the most of the time on the top of the cage, but sometimes ran about the aviary with the guineapigs and birds, and always squealed loudly with delight when I entered with fresh food.

Whether he incited the others to escape from their cage or not, I did not know; but one day I said to my father that his rats were very quiet, and had not been eating much, also that only one performer came out, and went round and round on his wheel, stopping occasionally and holding on to the bars with his pink feet as if to say, "Where are my brothers?"

I examined his cage, and found only three young ones in it; the other four were running loose in the aviary, probably to the great delight of the former solitary young one.

The other three soon got out, and now I had seven rats frisking to and fro over the earth floor of the aviary. They had a delightful time, stealing newspapers and straw from the guineapigs' barrels. They made a nice large nest in a hole in the earth, and for a time were model rats.

CHAPTER IX

FAREWELL TO THE RATS AND RABBITS

I got a little uneasy as the rats continued to grow, and to grow, and to grow. However, I reflected that they were not of pet stock. They were common sewer rats, and if they were a good size in the open, why should they not attain to a greater, here in this enclosure where they had not a care in the world, and had plenty of what must have been to them delectable food.

I had been accustomed to think of rats as dirty creatures, and was surprised to find how much they loved water, and with what determination they washed and brushed themselves each day. They were model pets in that respect, but I was disappointed to find that they did not grow tame and come about me. By this time they were enormous fellows, and at night I used to take a lantern and go into the aviary, and sit on a box and watch them. I wanted to love them. They were my pet rats. Why not grow as attached to them as to a dog or a cat? I could not. I would not let myself shudder as they passed to and fro near me, but I wanted to do so. They did not care particularly for me. I could see that in every movement of the big, sleek gray creatures, and they did not trust me. I felt badly to find that they were excavating a tunnel in the earth. I did not see them actually at it. They used to work on their fortifications at night, and every morning there would be a heap of earth piled up, with large stones too heavy for one rat to carry.

My father said that he would have liked immensely to see how they carried out those stones. I thought that this performance implied lack of confidence in me. What were the rats going to do there, and what did they expect me to do, that they deserted their shallow nest and made this underground cave? I did not know but what they had tunneled through to the street, but this fortunately they did not do. When the den was finished, they lined it, and retired to it, and I saw very little of them.

They might have been there to this day, if it had not been for the death of my robin, Dick, that I have already referred to. When I went into the aviary, and found that they had deliberately murdered a bird, when there was an abundance of food for them, I gave up my plan of reforming rats, and decided that as the fathers were, so will the children be, and they had better go back to the street.

The next morning my father went into the aviary with a workman, who carried a pick and shovel. Our two fox-terriers ran after them. Two rats escaped to the outer world, where I imagined them telling wonderful tales to their relatives of a basement where food and drink abounded, and where they had made a wheel spin round and round, and had tried to lead a good, respectable life, and had failed.

The fox-terriers pounced on the other five rats as they ran out from the snug home we found they had made by tunneling into an old French drain built alongside the house. I worried a little, thinking that perhaps they should all have been driven into the street, but have since found out more about rats, and accept the statement of many wise persons, who say that they carry disease germs, and should be exterminated. I would not torture them, but would kill them mercifully and speedily.

This common, grayish rat has had a remarkable history. Starting as far as we know from western China, he became a sailor rat, and has by means of ships gone all over the world, driving the black rat in terror before him.

The gray, or brown rat, as he is often called, will, in favorable situations, increase enormously, producing annually several litters, each of which may contain eight, ten, or even twelve or fourteen young ones.

Some years ago, the number of rats in the slaughter-houses about Paris was so great that as many as two and three thousand would be killed in a single night. However, they have friends. I have heard that in some mines the miners make great pets of rats, and are angry if any visitor brings his dog with him. The rats are the only creatures that willingly stay underground with the men, and beside acting as scavengers, their sharp eyes and ears are ever on the alert for slipping sand, or pebbles falling from the rocky roofs. They hear noises unperceived by the men, and previous to a caving-in, will run for the open air with wild squeals of terror. Small wonder that the miners protect them.

They have also admirers of their intelligence, among whom I am proud to number myself, for why should carnivorous human beings be too hard on rats for killing birds? However, as a family, we decided that the rat episode had been so painful that we could no longer have them about the house. Workmen were called in, and concrete floors were laid in furnace-room, coal-cellars, and storeroom. The poor rats were determined not to be driven out, and if the workmen left the concrete while it was soft, they would dig their way up again. I was not willing to cover the earth in the aviary, and there was no danger of the rats getting in there, unless they tunneled from the other side of the house. This they would be quite capable of doing, if they thought they could get into the aviary in that way, and to this day I never see holes in the earth, or freshly scratched places, without anxiously examining them for traces of my dreaded gray enemies.

After making up my mind that rats were not suitable inhabitants of an aviary, I decided that the next animals to go would be the rabbits; but first, I was to have some further experiences with them. The little girls who had brought me the two white rabbits came to see me shortly after the expulsion of the rats, and with mournful faces informed me that they were about to leave Halifax with their parents.

"And we were going to give you our three dear rabbits," they said earnestly, "but one died."

I tried hard to look regretful for this untimely death, and one of the little girls went on to say, "We put this rabbit, Venus, in a basket to bring to you, then we saw the basket heave. We opened it, and there was Venus with froth on her mouth. Now what did she die of? Was it from poison? We had given her some red leaves from the woods, but the other rabbits ate them, and they did not die."

"Perhaps her sister kicked her," said the other little girl.

"Anyway, it was a great shock to me," continued the first one disconsolately. "I howled from ten minutes past three till six—Venus would have had such a good time with you."

"Well, she is safely over her troubles now," I remarked, "and I am not particularly anxious to add to my stock of rabbits. I am becoming more interested in birds, and an old man came out the other day bringing me a half-sick rabbit."

The children at once asked to see this rabbit, and named him Raggylug for me. Then they walked to and fro in the furnace-room, never keeping still a minute, stubbing their toes on the floor, or leaning against the stone wall to talk of an astonishing number of subjects connected with animals, among others, their hatred of vivisection, and their intense hope that there would be immortality for animals.

"There must be animals in heaven," one of them said earnestly, "for are there not doves around the altar? and there must be cows and bees, if it is a land flowing with milk and honey."

Then, with an abrupt change, one of them said to me, "You must feel as if you were in heaven, Miss Saunders, when you get into this basement with all your animals."

In some embarrassment I replied that I did not consider the basement of my father's house an ideal place. Some day I hoped to have a better home for my birds.

However, I never said very much; for when those children talked, I always wanted to listen. Among all the animal-lovers that I have ever known, I never met with two more exquisitely thoughtful and sympathetic souls than these.

At that time they were absolutely torn with anxiety as to the fate of their two surviving rabbits, which I at last promised to take. They said, "We know they will be safe with you, Miss Saunders. But suppose anything should happen to you."

I told them over and over again, that if I were prematurely cut off, or had to part from my pets, measures would be taken to provide their rabbits with the best of homes.

One thing they strictly impressed upon me. They did not approve of cremation, and if their rabbits were to die, they must be buried in the ground.

"Our rabbits are so supernatural," one of them remarked.

To allay their intense anxiety, I promised everything they wished, and later on they brought the rabbits to me, both decorated with blue ribbon, and told me the larger one was Trixy Minerva, and the smaller one Candytuft Mercury. They said that Trixy was a saint, and was aunt to Candytuft, who was a sinner. Then they cut locks of hair from their pets' heads, took a painful farewell of them, and went away.

In some perplexity I surveyed my rabbit family after they left me. The gentle Raggylug was loping around the aviary. As Trixy bore a good character, I decided to put her in with him. Spotty and Rab would kill Candytuft Mercury if I turned him loose in the furnace-room, so I shut him and his blue ribbon up in a barrel, till I could think his case over.

The next morning I found that Trixy had bitten Raggylug's

ear, and the patient little fellow sat with a guineapig friend kindly licking the sore place for him. I hope it was sympathy, but I really believe that even model guineapigs may occasionally like the taste of blood.

I left Raggylug in the aviary for a further trial, and he soon learned that he must not gallop round at Trixy's heels. She did not like it.

What was I to do with Candytuft? That was now the burning question. He had to come out of that barrel, anyway. His little owners would be shocked if they should see him in it, so I turned him into the aviary and awaited developments.

They soon came. Delighted with his freedom, he stamped his soft paws on the earth, and bounded to and fro, making an occasional vicious onslaught on poor Raggylug, who hid behind the guineapigs' barrels.

This would not do. I must try a new combination, so I put Candy out in the furnace-room, and took Spotty in with Trixy. The usually good-natured Spotty flew at Trixy, kicked her, tore out great bunches of her hair, and in much trepidation I had to run and catch the furious Spotty, who was breathing spasmodically, and push the terrified Trixy in a corner to recuperate. She was twice his size, but he had beaten her. Now she would understand how Raggylug felt when she bit his ear.

I had forgotten that rabbits quarreled so much. When I was a girl my elder brother kept sixty of them together in a carriage-house loft, and in looking back, I could not remember hearing of the dreadful fights my few rabbits had had. My curiosity led me to interview him on the subject, and he laughed, and confessed that in his youthful days his loft was the scene of many woolly battles and hair-breadth escapes, when his boy friends brought their rabbits to pit against his.

I had to come back to my rabbit problem. As the days went by I was no nearer its solution. Trixy and Candy both whipped the model Raggylug. Trixy bit him, and Candytuft kicked him.

Candytuft also bit Trixy. Rab and Spotty bit and kicked all three. Finally, to give myself a breathing-spell, for I did not propose to spend the rest of my life in the basement, settling rabbit quarrels—they used to bite me too—I put Candy in a box.

The king of terrors, who solves so many problems, came to my rescue. One morning Lizzie ran upstairs and informed me that Spotty was "stiff."

I hurried down to him and finding him swollen enormously, I rushed castor oil down his throat, and got him into a hot bath. I was too late. He died—surprisingly strong and struggling to the last, though at first he was patient and quiet. Probably the bath was not a good thing. I was puzzled as to the cause of his death, until I found some decayed potatoes that had been put by the furnace to be burned.

We had a post mortem examination, and my supposition was found to be correct. Poor, inoffensive Spotty had been killed by greediness. I knew he had not been hungry, for I always had plenty of food lying about. I believe in giving pet creatures plenty of exercise and an abundance of food. I rarely find that they eat too much.

To my great uneasiness Trixy fell ill after this, and I was obliged to have recourse to my oil bottle. I felt thankful that the children could not see their fresh white beauty with her dejected air and oily, dirty face. This time I evidently did the right thing, for Trixy pulled through.

After I had had these rabbits a few months the time came for my trip to Europe, and I was not surprised to hear that my family would take care of my birds and guineapigs, but utterly refused to have anything to do with the quarrelsome rabbits.

I did not blame them. They had all been witnesses of amusing rabbit fights in which the two combatants would take their station opposite each other, warily watching to see which could get the first jump. The advantage was not to jump highest, but to jump first. The first one in the air as they came down, would give a dreadful kick with his hind legs at his opponent's body. So heating and so wearing was this form of contest, that in a few seconds the two combatants were completely overcome, and the air was full of kicked-off hair. Retiring to a little distance from each other, they would both lie flat on their stomachs on the cool earth, then, after a time, would rise for another round that I always promptly stopped.

I hope I am not too hard on the pretty creatures, but this particular set I had was very bad. When they had young ones they were worse than ever. A mother rabbit would viciously tear open the side of a baby rabbit belonging to another mother, and I have seen them snap at and try to kill young birds.

Raggylug, the only well-behaved one, was so bitten by Candytuft that he became afflicted by a huge swelling on the back of his head. One of the guineapigs found the niche between the swelling and the top of Raggylug's head a good resting-place, and it was amusing to see the little creature lying there, quite undisturbed by good, patient Raggy.

I put sulphur ointment on the swelling, but it did not improve; and I was just about to have him killed when, one day as he was sunning himself out in the garden, Candytuft rushed at him and despatched him.

It was almost impossible to keep the rabbits apart. They were as quick as dogs in leaping through open doors, and flying at each other. I made up my mind to scatter my rabbits, and found good homes for them all. I trembled when I thought of what the little girls would say, but I wrote them an apologetic and explanatory letter, and to my relief, they took the affair very philosophically.

I have never kept rabbits since; but if ever I had sufficient room, I would really enjoy having a few pairs of the pretty creatures—separate, not together.

CHAPTER X

A BIRD FROM OVER THE SEA

Shortly after parting from my rabbits and rats I became much interested in hearing from a naturalist friend, of the arrival of a strange bird on our coast. A pitiless gale had been beating strange birds shoreward, and this wanderer had been picked up, helpless, but still living. The man who found him knew from his brilliant coloring that he was no Nova Scotian bird, and sent a description of him to my naturalist friend, who at once pronounced him to be a purple gallinule—a heron-like wader related to the coot family.

"The bird is a native of the Gulf States," wrote the naturalist, "and of the South Atlantic generally. I wish he could give us an account of his trip. He must have been caught in a tyrannous blast, and been whirled more than a thousand miles, and he not a great flyer, either."

I was quite excited about this bird that had been hurried so swiftly through the air; the more so, as I heard that he was intended as a present for me, after he had recuperated in a cage that he seemed quite contented in.

Shortly afterward the naturalist arrived with the gallinule in a box, with a kind of chimney to it to accommodate his long neck. I could not see him properly in it, so we hurried to the aviary and let him loose on the earth. He was a beauty, with handsome blue and purple plumage, and seemed a gentle, reasonable sort of bird, not at all frightened by captivity. After eating gravely from a cup of cornmeal pudding, with worms for raisins, he took a long drink.

The guineapigs, devoured with curiosity, ran round and round this handsome bird with the long, slender legs. He walked very lame on one of these legs, but after examination, we decided that there was nothing broken—he had merely rheumatism in it.

In order to hasten his recovery I took him up to my warm study, where I added hard-boiled eggs to his bill of fare. These he liked very much. I loved to watch him. He had a pretty way of carrying his long neck and head, an exceedingly calm, philosophical manner, and lovely dark eyes. He had also a comical way of flirting his tail and showing the pretty white feathers in it.

After a few days his wings did not droop so much. He was getting better, his excellent appetite helping him in this respect. While eating, he was very economical; and if a crumb dropped outside his dish he at once picked it up.

Soon he began to fight his cage in my study, and beat himself about so much, that I decided to put him downstairs. First, though, we must take his photograph, and we had great amusement in arranging a sofa in a window, and persuading him to sit on it.

After his picture was taken, he was put into the aviary, and seemed delighted with the greater freedom, flying to and fro, with his legs sticking straight out behind him. Finally he calmed down, walked about, looked out the windows, and at night-time took possession of a broad, soft nest that I had made him in one of the trees standing against the wall. He liked the protection of these firs and spruces. Animals and birds kept in captivity enjoy having some place where they can get out of sight. I often pity squirrels kept in open cages. They should always have a box to run into.

The guineapigs kept on bothering the gallinule. When he was eating, they pressed close to him. He eyed them severely, but did not retaliate until they were actually on his long, slender claws. Then, with a well-directed blow, he would strike them exactly on the top of the head with his heavy beak, and I fear caused the death of several of them, that were found lying quite still and cold where they had fallen in their tracks.

He also disliked being bothered or troubled by any birds, and in a quiet but determined way always got rid of them. Shortly after I got him he took a fancy to double up his long legs, and squat in a nest of straw that I made for him on a broad window ledge. As he sat there in the sun, the other birds went to call on him. He paid no attention to first calls, but when the ringdoves, whose chosen place was near him, came a second time, he leaned over, took one by the tail, and pulled it.

This seemed to me to show some sense of humor, and I afterward noticed other birds indulging in tail-pulling. Canaries are particularly fond of it, and I often have seen a mischievous canary sneaking up to another who is sitting on a branch, his little throat distended, his head back. He is singing the most eloquent song he knows. Perhaps he is showing off before some pretty stranger whose good graces he wishes to gain, when, lo, he is thrown into a most pitiable state of confusion and contortion, for canary number one has seized his tail and has given it a good tweak.

He almost falls back, then with a wrathful squawk the song changes, and he pursues the bad bird to give him a pecking.

The gallinule never liked my ringdoves. I brought them home with me when I came from my European trip. I got them in Boston, though I had resolved to get them in Paris, for one day while walking down the Boulevard Montparnasse, I had fallen in love with a gentle bird that had called, "Coo, oo, oo!" to me, from the door of a laundry.

I turned to speak to him, as he stood bowing unceasingly to me, and the smiling proprietor of the shop informed me that he was very tame and never flew away.

"I shall have a pair of ringdoves when I go home," I remarked, and therefore purchased two pretty birds, and took them up to Nova Scotia with me. They were gentle birds, but unyielding and obstinate, and they did not want the gallinule in their corner of the aviary. The laundryman had been right about their love for home. They rarely wandered about the aviary, but kept in their pet place. The gallinule, forgetting how he had resented their visits, would insist on calling on them, and then there would be a fight.

Their combats were bloodless, and exceedingly funny. When the doves saw him approaching they would look angry, would slide along their perch, and, lifting their wings, would give him good, sound slaps. All the dove and pigeon tribe fight in this amusing way, and they can give quite hard blows.

The gallinule, finding one on each side of him, would try to look martial, and clapping his wings close to his sides, would tilt backward, double up his long legs, spread his claws flat, and give a splay-footed kick at them. He had the effect of falling over backward as he fought, and his doubling-up process must have been as fatiguing as it was funny, for he always brought it speedily to a close, and beating a retreat, left the doves in possession of their perch.

Before I leave these doves, I must speak of their amusing watchdog habit. All through the night they would cry out if they heard any noise inside the house. It would have been impossible for a burglar to enter the basement, without having them call loudly in concert to him, "Coo-oo, ooo-ooo! Whooo!"

After I had had Beauty for some months, I had another gallinule come over seas and land to join my collection of birds, though he, of course, had not the least intention of entering an aviary when he left the sunny South. Strange to relate, he too was picked up exhausted on the shores of Nova Scotia, but nearer to me, having dropped down close to Dartmouth, a town across the harbor from Halifax.

I first heard of him from a bird-fancier in Dartmouth, who called on me and asked me what I gave my gallinule to eat.

"You have not by any chance a live one?" I asked.

He said he had; that a little boy had picked up a strange bird on the railroad track by the shore, and knowing that this gentleman had a fine collection of stuffed birds, had brought it to him, asking him to kill and mount it for him.

Telling the boy that it would be a pity to kill so handsome a bird, the gentleman gave him a dollar, and told him to choose one of his already stuffed birds.

The boy went away happy, and the gentleman came to me to write a bill of fare for the stranger, as he wished very much to keep him.

I told him I had not dreamed there were any but stuffed gallinules for several hundreds of miles near me, and that as his bird was fortunate enough to be alive, I would recommend a general sort of diet, for I saw my Beauty picking at all sorts of food in the aviary.

Above all, we must have a good, deep water dish. No matter how cold the weather was, Beauty would stand for hour after hour in his bathtub, gazing about him in a quiet contemplative fashion, and occasionally making a swift bob down into the water to wet his purple plumage.

The gentleman said he would possibly get tired of keeping a solitary bird, and if he did, would send it over to me. Therefore, I was not surprised, when in a few days gallinule number two arrived in a basket. Once more I was excited. What would the meeting be like between these two wanderers from a foreign shore? Imagine my delight if, held prisoner in Mexico, I should suddenly have thrust into my prison another real, live Nova Scotian.

I took the new bird down to the aviary and let him out. He also was a handsome bird, and in good condition, in spite of his long flight; and was, I imagined, slightly larger than mine.

To my disappointment, there were no hysterics, no heroics

about the meeting. They did not fly to meet each other. My gallinule looked at the strange gallinule, and the strange gallinule looked at him. I thought I saw tokens of quiet pleasure on the part of each one, but it was extremely quiet.

The stranger, after gazing about him with the cool philosophical stare that seems to be peculiar to gallinules, walked up to a little looking-glass, and pecked at his reflection there. As it did not reciprocate, he kicked at it scornfully. Then he looked about to see what there was to eat. After satisfying his appetite he had a bath.

The next day I found him stuffing himself with bread and milk that was very warm, almost hot. I was struck by it, for most birds like their food lukewarm or cold.

Though still undemonstrative, he soon attached himself to my gallinule, and they usually kept together, though their friendship was of the coolest, calmest kind. Nothing ever disturbed the equanimity of those gallinules but the firing of the twelve o'clock gun from the citadel in the middle of the city. In all colonial towns around the world that possess an English garrison this noontide gun or cannon is fired.

The first gallinule always jumped and gave a loud squawk when it went off. The other one did not mind it so much.

CHAPTER XI

GOOD-BYE TO THE GALLINULES

Not long after the entrance of this new gallinule into my bird world, circumstantial evidence convicted him of a crime that seemed to me particularly atrocious and unnecessary.

I had bought two little birds—a linnet and a goldfinch. These birds came with large numbers of other birds from Europe to New York, which is the great market for foreign birds.

They were both so restless in the cage in which I put them for quarantine purposes, that I was convinced they were trapped birds. This suspicion was confirmed by finding some of the linnet's feathers stuck together with bird lime. Indeed, he was in such a state that I did not see how he had maintained enough freedom of movement to get about the large cage in which I had put him. I cut off the sticky feathers, felt angry with his trappers for catching him, for the little wild creature beat himself against his bars all the time, and I let him loose in the aviary. He flew about the basement, ascended to the roof-veranda, made friends with one of my native linnets— so-called, which are really finches, and finally I gave him his freedom. He flew away with the finch, and I hope migrated with him.

This European linnet was a quiet-looking, dark bird. The goldfinch was utterly different, both in appearance and in disposition, and was also totally unlike our pretty, bright American goldfinch. The English bird was about five inches long, his whitish beak was conical and sharp, his feet were brown and slender, the front of his head was bright scarlet, the top of it black. His cheeks and upper neck were pure white, the sides of his breast light brown, the middle whitish gray, his wing feathers were velvety black, yellow, and white. In Europe he and his fellows are of great service to farmers, their sharp little beaks dragging many insects from their hiding-places. One of their chief articles of diet is thistle-seed, and they are trapped by means of bird lime placed near bunches of thistles.

My little goldfinch did not seem very strong. One can fancy that after having a struggle with limed twigs, and then being shut up in a tiny cage with an entire change of food, and being transported across a wide ocean, he would not to any sensible degree find himself benefited in health. This poor little fellow soon died, and the bird-dealer gave me another one that worried along through one winter and spring. He was like the first one, as far as two birds can be alike. I became very fond of him. He was such a quiet, good little creature, and never molested another bird. When moulting-time came his weak points were accentuated. His feathers seemed to drop out all at once, and he lost his ability to fly. However, he bore his affliction philosophically, and seeing that his wings had deserted him, calmly took to his slender brown feet. Through the long, pleasant autumn days, he would go from tree to tree, climbing from one branch to another till he reached the top, then at night he always chose for his bed-place a perch near the old-fashioned worked picture, given to my father by one of his parishioners, and entitled, "Sweet rest in Heaven."

This picture hung in my bedroom, a sunny apartment opening on the roof-veranda. I had very much enjoyed this room, but my birds had become so sociable, hopping in to see me, examining my pincushion and workbasket for threads and bits of cloth for their nests, and also crowding me so much when I tried to look in my mirror, that for a part of the year I gave the room up to them and slept in another.

I had nailed some branches and perches to the walls and

the little goldfinch when morning came, carefully picked his way down from behind the picture, and began journeying to and fro on the veranda, with many slips and many falls, but with so much enjoyment of his liberty that I could not bear to shut him up in one of the detested cages.

I knew that it was scarcely safe to have this little crippled fellow wandering about among large birds, but he was so discreet, and the large birds seemed so forbearing, that I hoped nothing would happen to him.

Then I was with my birds nearly all day long, either on the veranda or in the bird-room, and if I were not there some members of the family would be reading, sewing, or entertaining friends out in the sunshine.

I kept for several years from eighty to a hundred birds at a time, and there were a good many quarrels which would be quickly settled by a word from us, or sometimes by the birds themselves.

I have often seen a bird rush between two others who were angrily beating each other. Of course, the purpose of this bird is not to settle the quarrel. After watching them carefully I concluded that they interfere from a variety of motives, none of them altruistic. I think the chief reason of their interference arises from the fact that birds are highly sensitive creatures. They hate sharp noises and any disturbance. If they do not understand a noise they fly away and hide, or rush wildly to and fro. If they do understand it, as in the case of two of their fellows quarreling, they irritably interfere, as if to say, "Why do you make such a horrible noise and disturb the harmony of things?"

The gallinules loved the roof-veranda, and solemnly ascending the elevator, would stand for hours in the water dishes, or would bask in the sunlight. I noticed that they moved about a good deal at night, and I have since heard that there is more movement in the bird world at night than we sometimes suppose.

I know many of my birds would make their way about, if there was the least particle of light, and some of them would arouse me by flying to and fro, and singing, if the moonlight were bright.

I did not know very much about gallinules, and it did not occur to me that they would prey upon birds, though I did find one of them playing with one of the turtles. However, gallinules were waders, and anything that lived in the water would be legitimate prey. But this second gallinule should not have killed my dear little goldfinch, and torn his wise little head from his shoulders.

This was the painful sight that greeted me one morning as I stepped out to the veranda. There was the headless body. There stood the gallinule, looking as if he were thinking of nothing but the beauty and brightness of the morning.

How did I know this gallinule, Beauty Number Two, was to blame? Well, if a mother has a certain number of children, and studies the character of each one, she knows them as thoroughly as one created being can understand another. She leaves the children in a room and returns to find one hurt and crying. She looks around, and by certain indefinable signs discovers the aggressor.

The gallinule's philosophical, uninterested air might have led an outsider astray, and for just a very short time my suspicions did wander to a cardinal bird. However, they came back to the long-legged bird, and after a time I saw him playing with the poor little goldfinch's head. I put him through the gate leading to the elevator, and told him to stay in regions below for a time. I would not have a murderer above. He did not like this, and with his companion would come and stand at the gate, pleading to be let in, until at last I relented; and whether he understood or not, he did not kill another bird for a long time.

When I moved the birds to my farm in the country, the gallinules went too. In an ell of the house were some rooms with screened windows. The screen on one door was loose, and my first gallinule managed to insinuate his body, and get out one fine day.

Below the house was a meadow, and through the meadow ran a beautiful little river. We could hear the birds the farmers called meadow-hens laughing down there all day long, and at night the legions of frogs kept up an harmonious chant of "Rain, rain, rain!"

Along the river banks were lovely wild flowers and thick shrubbery. I imagined that the gallinule would have a delightful time in this dense covert, and as he had been clever enough to find his way to Nova Scotia from Mexico or Georgia, perhaps, when autumn came, he might be clever enough to find his way back. So I took the other gallinule and carried him out to the bank overhanging the meadow. I threw him high up in the air, and he sank down from my sight among the violets and long grass of the hillside.

From what I knew of his habits, I concluded that he would hide there till night came, then make his way to the river. I hoped that he would find Beauty Number One, and many times since I have thought that I would give a very great deal to know the ultimate fate of my two gallinules.

CHAPTER XII

FIRST ACQUAINTANCE WITH PIGEONS

Soon after starting my aviary in Halifax, I began to think of keeping pigeons. I had always admired the tame birds about the streets, but I had never studied them. I knew nothing whatever of their habits, except that I had once heard a woman whose husband kept a stable, say that it was perfectly surprising to see the way in which great fat young pigeons that had grown to be as large as their parents, would follow these same parents about and make them put food down their throats.

Some one told me of a young man who kept fancy pigeons in Halifax, and one day my sister and I called on him. His birds were mostly white, and as I stood looking at this first collection of pigeons that I had ever intelligently examined, I was conscious of a feeling almost of ecstasy. Only those persons who are bird-lovers can understand this peculiar delight in the mere contemplation of the restless, beautiful creatures.

Birds arouse certain emotions, and touch a certain set of feelings that no other creature has power to stir. They are so beautiful, so finished, so fragile and elegant, and so helpless. Baby birds always remind me of human babies. The young of many animals will nose about and search for food. The tiny bird does nothing but open its beak. You might kill it—it cannot resist, but its helplessness is its chief claim to your love and protection.

In connection with the protective instinct of bird-lovers for birds, I was interested in hearing of a certain popular English general, who is said to have worried incessantly, not over the human beings that he had killed when fighting in defense of his country, but over the death of a helpless lizard that he one day thoughtlessly struck down with his walking-stick. He was strong, and the lizard was weak; and instead of protecting it, he killed it.

Possibly with regard to pigeons, I am too enthusiastic; but after keeping some hundreds of birds, and being devoted to them all, I prefer over and over again the bird we have always with us—the domesticated pigeon.

My first pair were fantails—white ones that my sister chose from the young man's collection, and gave to me for a Christmas present. I used to spend hours in watching them. Their tip-toeing walk, their convulsive jerking and twitching of the neck and chest, and gently bouncing heads, were intensely interesting, and not painful to witness, as they seemed to enjoy their bodily peculiarities. However, much as I liked them, I would class them among the monstrosities in pigeon breeds. I prefer a straight bird to a deformed one. The only consolation was that they had never known anything different.

"That fellow lives pretty much in the back of his house," said a man, who once stood gazing at a fantail.

Their appetites amused me, and I was informed that a pigeon is capable of eating in a day a quantity more than equal to its own weight, though fanciers estimate that one-tenth of a pound is a sufficient daily amount.

Their manner of drinking was also a revelation to me, and illustrated the lack of accurate observation in the average person. How many times I had noticed pigeons about the streets of cities, but now, for the first time, I was to find out how they drank.

I used to amuse myself by saying to my friends, "How do pigeons drink?"

Nearly every one answered, "I don't know. Like a chicken, I suppose."

"They drink as we do," I used to respond, with pride in my superior information. "They thrust their bills into the water, and keep them there till they have had enough."

My fantails were very fond of bathing in a big pan that I gave them, and used to keep their red feet beautifully clean. At night they did not go on a perch, but crouched on some projecting bricks in the wall.

After a time I concluded that pigeons liked a flat surface to sleep on, so I got some boxes from our grocer, had the fronts knocked out, except one strip to confine the newspaper and straw I put in, and hung them on the wall.

The pigeons were delighted with them. They would fly inside the boxes, step about on the straw, coo excitedly, then would fly up on the flat tops and go to sleep.

Later on, when I got more pigeons, I found these big cracker boxes far more agreeable to them than nesting-pans. The female when setting, likes the protection of the covered top and enclosed sides. Then the male can always sleep above her, and hear her every movement, and he never allows any other bird to alight on his particular box. To clean them, I would roll up newspaper and straw lining and put in the furnace, then set the box aside to be whitewashed.

I usually kept vermin powder in the nests, and never was troubled with parasites. Clean bedding is absolutely essential for healthy creatures. Many persons say that birds are dirty. So is every created thing dirty that is not kept clean. Even when I had young pigeons I could clean the nests. I would warm a newspaper on the furnace for delicate birds, put a bunch of soft hay on it, carefully lift the little birds on it, and slip them in the box. The parents rarely resented my interference.

I must add to this that fanciers who keep large numbers of pigeons, and who do not change their nest linings as often as I do, never use hay and straw. Red nits crawl into the hollow stalks and breed freely. Tobacco stems and pine shavings are the nesting materials used, and birds are often allowed to make their own nests.

Pigeons kept in captivity do not usually lay eggs in winter, if they are kept in a cold place. If they are in a warm loft, they will lay eggs and rear young ones, but most fanciers separate the male from the female birds at the beginning of the winter. The spring and summer are enough for the raising of young ones.

I knew that my aviary was warm enough for the pigeons to lay in, and wondered why they did not do so. They fussed about the nest, giving each other resounding slaps with their wings, and finally the fancier discovered that he had not given me a pair, so he changed them, and I got two buff fantails instead.

These were two quiet, businesslike birds, and soon I found two eggs in one of the nests. The mother sat on them from four or five in the afternoon until about ten the next morning. Then, if her mate did not fly to the nest, she would groan ominously. He always hurried to her when she showed this sign of temper, and bowing and cooing prettily, would step patiently on the eggs.

The female would stretch her wings, shake herself, pick off the loose flakes of skin that pigeons shed like dust, trip around the aviary to see what there was for breakfast, stuff herself well, take a long drink, and perhaps a bath, then would sit in any ray of sunlight she could find.

The male bird had to stick to his post till five o'clock came. Then Mrs. Pigeon went back for the night. This was kept up for eighteen days, until my mother, who was a constant visitor to the aviary, reported at the breakfast table that she had found half an eggshell on the ground. I was quite excited about this news that meant the first bird had been hatched in my aviary. I hurried downstairs, and saw the buff pigeon fly off the nest with another half eggshell in her bill. She did not drop it near the nest, but took it to the other end of the aviary, making me wonder whether this was the survival of the habit of wild pigeons that would not want an enemy to find a shell near them, lest it might lead to the discovery of the young birds.

The instinct of birds is a wonderful thing. I am often amused in watching my canaries eat. For over three hundred years they have been domesticated birds, yet they never keep their heads down while eating. There is the dab at the seed, then the quick glance about, I suppose from the old habit of never for one instant giving up the guard against an enemy.

After I saw the mother pigeon fly back to her nest I approached it, and tried to push her aside, so that I might see what she had in there. She was in a terrible rage, exclaimed at my impertinence, and struck me so fiercely with her wing that I waited till the father pigeon went on at ten o'clock. He was very reasonable, and allowed me to look at his treasure, which was more like a tiny yellow blind worm than anything else. However, he was as proud of it as if it had been fully fledged, and whenever it lifted its wobbling head, would pump some breakfast down its tiny throat.

The large crop of the pigeon becomes glandular during the breeding season, and secretes a milky fluid that softens the partly digested food on which the young are fed. This young fellow being alone—the other egg did not amount to anything—was so well stuffed that he soon became as fat as a lump of butter, and down began to appear on his wings.

I was very much interested in seeing him fed. The father pigeon would take the young one's beak crosswise in his own, and pull out its neck as if it were made of rubber, and then send the milky fluid gurgling down his throat. When the young one had had enough, he would put his head under the parent's breast. The father or mother would survey him closely, and if the squab raised his head in the slightest degree they would again try to feed him.

In a short time his eyes opened, and very pretty yellowish eyes they were. He had a big bill that reminded me of a duck, and the enterprising little creature actually snapped this bill at me when I went near the nest. He became covered with dark yellow pin feathers, and his fat body was almost hot to the touch. He breathed with great rapidity, and his mother soon gave up sitting on him at night, and perched near-by. Sometimes I felt afraid that he might be cold, and would push her toward him. She always grumbled at me, and soon I came to the conclusion that a mother pigeon knew better how to bring up a young one than I did. When the squab became fully fledged the mother drove him from the nest, and laid two more eggs in it. The young fellow, considerably surprised, and uncommonly shaky on his legs, hurried to his father, and trotted up and down the aviary with him.

The father, who was perfectly devoted to him, was now a pretty busy bird. Several times before ten every morning he had to look sharply about to see where were the best seeds for his own and his young one's breakfast. Then he had to stuff his crop, and grunting amiably, walk to a water dish, and take a good long pull at it, for pigeons are heavy drinkers, particularly when feeding their young. All the time he was doing this I used to think that his nerves would certainly give out, for the fat young one was waddling about close to him, flapping his wings, and screaming for food as desperately as if he had had nothing to eat for days instead of minutes.

When the father was all ready, he would let the young one thrust his bill in his, then they would both shut their eyes, and the old work of pumping down the breakfast would go on. But now, if the young one thought he had not had enough, he would run all about the aviary after his father, cornering and enclosing him with his flapping great wings, and shrieking spasmodically, "More, more!" After a time he always quieted down, and took his morning stroll with his father about the aviary. Now that he had left the nest, he was no longer a squab,

but a squeaker. When his father went to "spell" the mother, to
let her have a run, pidgie would settle down near-by and have
a nap. He really seemed to be fonder of his father than of his
mother and—though, as I have said before, we must struggle
against the tendency to humanize birds too closely—the father
seemed to be fond of him.

CHAPTER XIII

THE HOMING PIGEON THE KING OF BIRDS

One day when the poor little squeaker, in attempting to fly, got one leg over the perch and could go neither forward nor backward, and hung with flapping wings, the father flew to his relief and helped him over.

No one knows until he has carefully observed birds, what untiring labor is required in bringing up young ones. The parents do nothing else but feed and watch their nestlings. Every bird seems to have the firm conviction that he is in the world for the purpose of raising healthy young ones, and as many as possible. He makes his nest, raises a brood, pushes them off in the world, makes another nest, raises another brood, and so on, until he is removed to bird paradise.

If human beings gave as much attention to the raising of their young, we should have an almost perfect race. However, we would scarcely lift sick young ones out of the nest to die. In that respect we are ahead of our bird friends. We might imitate them in one respect, and that is in the way they seem to prevent sick and delicate birds from becoming heads of families. I have noticed that ailing birds in my aviary, in some way or other, do not wish, or are not allowed to have mates.

One handsome but delicate canary never seeks a mate, but all day long flies by his father's side. He is quite an old bird, but he never leaves this little yellow father, night nor day. The father makes nests, raises young ones, and flies about, always with his devoted trailer.

While my buff pigeons grew and prospered, and raised other young ones, I got another pair in rather a peculiar way. Being in town one morning I stepped into an auctioneer's room, and there, in a cage, saw a pair of homing pigeons looking very disconsolate. I inquired what their history might be, and the auctioneer said that a passenger on a steamer that had lately come into our fine harbor from England, had brought the birds with him, and on leaving the train for Northwestern Canada, had left the birds behind him.

"What a strange thing to do," I remarked, as I looked at the traveling-cage and the pretty little drinking dish. Why did he suppose a man would undergo the expense of bringing birds on a long voyage from England and then drop them half-way to his destination?

The auctioneer said he would give it up, and then I further remarked that the cake crumbs in the box were not proper food for pigeons.

He said he knew it, and he wished I would buy them.

I asked him how much he wanted for them, and he said he had no idea how much they were worth, but I might have them for one dollar and seventy-five cents.

I had begun to read and inquire about pigeons, and knew there were many fancy breeds—fantails, pouters with long necks and globular crops, jacobins with their big hoods, snake-like magpies, short-faced tumblers and long-faced tumblers, tipplers, dragoons, swallows, owls, and many other kinds, but I did not know what the prices ought to be.

If these birds were trained homers, or working homers, as they are called, they would be worth more than one dollar and seventy-five cents. However, the auctioneer could not assure me of this, so I paid him the money, and sent the birds home.

It was touching to see the pleasure they took in getting out of their cage. They ate and drank and bathed and ran their pink tongues over the lumps of rock-salt I kept about. Nearly every bird I had, even canaries, would peck eagerly at this salt, though caged canaries would die if fed salt.

These two pigeons flew to the roof-veranda, and as soon as I discovered their preferred corner I gave them a box in it. There they laid not two but four eggs, and sat on them, one relieving the other, after the usual intervals. I was very proud and very boastful, until after I had a call from my friend the pigeon-fancier, who laughed heartily at my two birds.

"They are females," he said, "a pair only lays two eggs for a nest." This threw some light on the strange actions of the Englishman. The birds had probably laid four eggs in their traveling-cage, and in disgust at finding that he had two females sold to him instead of a pair that would have enabled him to raise young ones, he had decided not to give them a further trip of a few thousand miles.

The fancier exchanged one of them for me, and I got a fine blue homer, who took kindly to my gray one, and soon raised a number of healthy, handsome birds. I became very fond of these homers, and on learning something of the history of their kind, soon surveyed them with feelings of mingled admiration and respect.

They are our best and most wonderful birds, and they were our first, for did not one of them perform the first messenger service on record in carrying the sprig of green to the waiting Noah in the ark?

The dove was the ancestor of the carrier—and the smerle and the cumulet and the carrier were the ancestors of the homer, and yet even to-day there are persons who do not know what a remarkable part pigeons play in times of peace, in times of war, and in times of love.

Ever since the days of Noah this chunky, round-headed, clear-sighted, faithful, intelligent little creature has been the hard-working servant of many nations. The Romans used him in war-time for conveying messages from the armies, and an old song tells us of a warrior wounded in battle sending an outpouring of his heart to his lady-love by means of a carrier pigeon:

> Fly away to my native land, sweet bird,
> Fly away to my native land;
> And bear these lines to my lady-love,
> I have traced with a feeble hand.
> She marvels much at my long delay,
> A rumor of death she has heard,
> She thinks, perhaps, I have falsely strayed;
> Fly away to her bower, sweet bird.

I read in a book about pigeons that, when Brutus was besieged in Mutina 43 b. c. by Mark Antony, by setting free carrier pigeons that flew over the heads of the besiegers and defied the blockade, he communicated with the Roman consuls who came to raise the siege.

A certain shrewd Mohammedan ruler of Syria and Egypt who reigned in a. d. 1145 had a pigeon postal service from one end of his dominions to the other. Towers were built for the protection of the little messengers, and from these towers watchmen strained their eyes to see that no hostile power attacked the birds in the service of the monarch.

To-day, in spite of telegraphy, telephones, and wireless communication, the brave birds hold their own. They are the messenger-boys of the air. Let us mention some of the errands they do.

They carry stock reports from large cities to the suburban residences of their owners. Ocean steamers carry them out to take last messages back. A lady in Boston once told me that she traveled through Europe and back again with a homing pigeon in her care. This valuable homer had been given to her in a basket, as the steamer left Boston. She was to release it when one day out. A thick fog came on, and as a fog is a deadly enemy to the brave little homer, she had to give him a trip abroad.

In Europe the end of a yacht race or a horse race is the signal for the release of a flock of homers, who carry the news to private lofts or newspaper offices.

While Gladstone was on his famous Midlothian campaign, homing pigeons carried reports from the different mining villages to Edinburgh. In the seclusion of their traveling-baskets the homers patiently awaited the conclusion of each speech of Gladstone's at political meetings, and as soon as the last words had left the speaker's lips, the reporters fastened their tiny slips to the birds' leg-bands—for every pigeon has a ring slipped on when he is only a few days old—and gently opening the baskets, allowed them to fly up into the air.

Up, up, still farther went the keen-sighted birds, circling again and again to get their bearings, then off in the direction of their home-lofts in Edinburgh, where tempting food, fresh water, and their loved nest-mates were awaiting them.

Had these home-lofts been at the South Pole they would still have started for them. To reach home or die is the pigeon's motto, and thousands, nay millions of them have perished for "home, sweet home."

Pigeons have several enemies. There is the cruel gunner waiting for them, and the dreaded hawk, that Chinese ingenuity circumvents by attaching shrill whistles to the tail feathers of certain of their homers. As the birds pass swiftly through the air the whistles blow and the hawks will not come near.

Then there are storms and variable winds, and often the birds' overpowering sense of fatigue, for many fanciers give their homers cruelly long journeys to perform. What a temptation to a weary bird perching on a tree branch, to rest himself for a few minutes, to go with a strange pigeon who so politely invites him to his near-by loft, where he will find rest and refreshment.

I have often read with interest advertisements in English bird newspapers of homing pigeons in strange lofts. "So-and-so could have his property if he would tell the initials and number on the leg-band of a certain bird, and also pay the expressage on the roamer." I think the foggy climate is largely to blame for these numerous lost birds. In a fog a pigeon must stop. He has nothing to guide him on his journey. Darwin, who studied these birds for twenty years, proved in the first place that their memory is phenomenal, and in the second, that their eye-sight is limited by the horizon only.

The United States, following the example of European governments, started some years ago an extensive system of lofts in the army and navy. Professor Marion, of the Naval Academy at Annapolis, Maryland, really began the organization of the messenger pigeon service for use in time of war.

Lieutenant Harlow, U. S. N., also started experiments at Key West, and when hostilities with Spain broke out, the navy department found on inquiry that Uncle Sam had a number of well-trained little war-birds at his disposal. Lieutenant Harlow's cote at Key West being only ninety miles from Havana, the birds had not long distances to fly. In every boat of the torpedo flotilla taken out to sea, these pacific, patient birds had their own quarters. They were released at intervals, and scarcely one pigeon failed to return to its cote at Key West, with its cipher message in the national water-tight message holder fastened on its leg.

These patriotic birds are equally ready for peaceful campaigns, if one can call a presidential election by that name. Once, during a hotly contested election in Arizona, they did fine service in bringing the returns for outlying districts, some of them flying at the rate of a mile a minute.

France is very suspicious of foreign-trained homers, since

her experience during the Franco-Prussian War. At that time she learned the great service done by pigeons in bringing relief to beleaguered Paris. Now she does foreign pigeons the honor of excluding them from France. An alien pigeon cannot take up its residence there except under such restrictions as any well-brought-up bird would resent.

Germany too has its pigeons. While traveling in that country I was amused at the military aspect of many of its inhabitants, and was not surprised to learn that it has military pigeons. One can imagine the proud carriage of a German war-bird.

CHAPTER XIV

PRINCESS SUKEY

The little kingdom of Belgium waxes most enthusiastic over pigeons. This is the great breeding center, this is the real home of the modern, thoroughbred homer. Pigeon-flying is the national pastime. One-fifth of the entire population are active fanciers, and their wonderful birds are sent away in such numbers that special trains are made up for them.

Why should it not be a national sport in America? One can think of no class of persons who would not be benefited by taking an interest in these most lovable and intelligent of birds. I have proved by my own experience that it is a delightful relief to turn from the strenuous fatigue of a modern day's work to the quiet of a pigeon-loft. Here are hard workers, but they are quiet, calm, reposeful.

Some famous trips have been made by American birds, though, as the number of lofts increases, the tendency is not to fatigue birds by too long a journey. Five hundred mile one-day records are made, but they are not very frequent. Homers can, however, fly much farther than five hundred miles. One owned by Mr. Samuel Hunter, of Fall River, Mass., flew home from Montgomery, Ala., a distance of over one thousand miles, and two homing pigeons lately arrived in their loft in Boston, Mass., greatly exhausted by a trip from Minneapolis. They had flown about twelve hundred miles.

Homers are especially valuable for physicians with a large country practice. They are faithful and trustworthy medical messengers. The doctor leaves a pigeon with a sick patient. In a few hours it can be released and will return to its physician-owner with the latest account of the condition of his patient.

One medical man relates in a book about pigeons a charming story of a child patient who was ill with fever. The doctor had left, and the child sat with his arm around the basket containing the pigeon messenger, who was quietly waiting till the time came for him to be sent to report the boy's condition to his master.

The mother, to interest her child, related the story of the dove that Noah sent from the ark. To her delight the bird in the story and the bird in the basket combined to soothe the child, who presently fell asleep with a smile on his weary face. He was better, and the birds had helped him.

While pigeons are excellent pets, and a means of relaxation for weary persons, I hold that of all classes to be benefited by their study and care I would put first boys and girls. Taking care of pigeons is easy work. They are hardy creatures, and books as to their management can be easily obtained. Nothing keeps a boy out of mischief like a loft of pigeons. Let him have homers by all means, rather than the elegant fancy pigeon monstrosities that care to do little but strut about a loft. Let him train his birds and have his traveling-basket to send them on railway journeys. Arrangements can be made with railway officials to release them at a given point.

The latest news that I can get of homing pigeons is from the Paris correspondence of the London "Standard."

It seems that the French authorities in the African Congo district have had some trouble in communicating with each other. They could not keep up a telegraph system, for mischievous natives delighted in cutting down telegraph poles, and in using them for firewood. Wild elephants also amused themselves by uprooting one pole after another. Wireless telegraphy could not be practised on account of the tropical atmosphere often charged with electricity, and generally saturated with moisture.

What was the French government to do? A pigeon post was

suggested, and they started with a main pigeon depot of one hundred birds at Brazzaville, and will have a chain of stations at a distance of about twenty-five miles. The chances of a bird being killed or going astray are put down at two per cent., so that a message sent over a hundred miles by four pigeons would have ninety-two chances out of a hundred of reaching its destination. A message of extra importance would be sent in duplicate by two birds. Besides the use of these pigeons for regular postal service, it is planned that travelers, explorers, and military scouts will also carry a few.

One other item of interest about homers I find in a late newspaper: A bird was released from a balloon over Dover, Vt., eight thousand five hundred feet in the air, and above the clouds. The earth was invisible, but the homer in a short time arrived safely at its Fall River cote.

Now, after all my praise of the hard-working, clean-shaped homing pigeon, I must make the confession that the favorite bird in my aviary—the one that I am perhaps foolishly fond of, is not a homer, but a monstrosity. However, there is a reason for my fondness for her, and I will relate the peculiar circumstances that endeared her to me.

I had obtained a pair of ruffed, elegant jacobins, and they had settled down in the box of straw I gave them, and had hatched two tiny squabs. One morning later I found one of these squabs a short distance from the nest. I picked it up and examined it. It had one deformed wing, and had either perished in the nest, or had been gently lifted out to die on the bare ground. I suspect the latter explanation was correct, for the next morning on going into the aviary I found the other squab on the ground. It was opening and shutting its beak painfully, and was evidently just gasping its last. I ran to the furnace-room and laid its cold body on the warm iron.

Then I examined it. There was nothing in its crop, and its little yellow, languishing body was thin and miserable. I took it upstairs, wrapped it up, and put it on a hot water bag, then gave it some bread and milk. The only way I could get the little exhausted creature to eat was by putting its feeble beak to my mouth and letting it take the food from between my half-closed teeth.

When night came I was puzzled to know what to do with it. I did not seem to realize the finality of the parent birds' act in putting a young one out of the nest, and carefully arranging a cloth nest on a hot water bag, so that it would not die of cold, even if the mother refused to sit on it, I took it down to the aviary and put it with its parents.

Of course, they did not go near it, and in the morning I found my pigeon again apparently drawing its last breath. I hurried it upstairs, and it did not go down again. I made it a bed in a little basket, and kept it near me night and day. It was powerfully ugly, and the family teased me a good deal about my pigeon, but I told them I had made a vow to save its life. I tried a good many experiments in feeding it, and very often in the middle of the night I would spring up and look at the basket to see if the little delicate creature were still alive.

Later on I learned how to bring up young pigeons successfully, but this one I almost killed by giving wrong food to it. I found later that a mixture of rolled oats, bread crumbs, and a few drops of milk and water—the whole made very fine and soft, agreed well with it. I got a medicine-dropper and a syringe, but for some time it would only eat from between my teeth or my fingers, this being the nearest approach to the parents' beak. After a while I made different kinds of grain and seeds into pills and slipped them down its throat. The bird soon became very tame, and would flap its wings and scream for food whenever it saw me. It was dubbed Princess Sukey by my sister, but for some time she was a ridiculous looking princess. I found she had a form of indigestion, and as she has had this ever since, I fancy that her parents, discovering this, had made up their minds that she was not worth bringing up.

A curious thing happened as soon as she opened her eyes. The young pigeons in the aviary always hissed at human beings who went near them. Princess Sukey, on account of her upbringing, looked upon human beings as her friends, and when I showed her a bird for the first time, she rose up in her nest, clapped her beak, and hissed in terror.

She hated birds, and has hated them ever since. One day, when she was a plump young pigeon, her father walked up to her, bowing and scraping as polite pigeons do. I was greatly amused to see Sukey take him by the long neck feathers and give him a good shaking. She had made up her pigeon mind to give birds the go-by and join her lot with me and my family, for she liked all of us, though I was her chief favorite, as I represented her food supply.

This father of hers was rather an inconstant bird. Once, when his own mate was very much in need of his services to help her in bringing up young ones, he left her to play with a lively, attractive pigeon, called Fanny Fantail. This Fanny was a bird without a mate, and a lonely male or female pigeon, or any other kind of bird, makes more trouble in an aviary than half a dozen pairs. I had to separate her from the jacobin before he would go back to his own nest.

For months Sukey was one of the ugliest birds that I ever saw. She had a long, poor crop of feathers on her body, but her big hood did not develop until she was full-grown. Her bare neck, ugly head, and yellowish eyes, made her a kind of laughing-stock, but soon there was a transformation. The blue blood in her told, and when her lovely red and white feathers did start, she was a beauty. It was the story of the ugly duckling over again. Her superb indifference to birds amused us greatly. Through the summer she followed me about the roof-veranda, sat in my room with me, or waited patiently for me if I went out. During my absence she would sometimes attach herself to some other member of the family. She was very fond of playing with me. She would sit on my shoulder, and run her beak over my ear and cheek; and if I were reading, she would peck the leaves of my book. If I sewed, she caught my thread and sometimes so bothered me that I would put her out of the room and shut the door. Then she was in distress, and would trot up and down the window ledge outside, tapping the glass with her beak, and pleading eloquently to be allowed in again.

The veranda was alive with birds, but she paid no attention to them, unless one of them came near her, to have a sly peep in the tiny mirror on the window ledge. Any such presuming bird, if she could catch it, she would beat thoroughly. She had no curiosity about new things, except human beings. One day I placed her in front of a horned toad, and my sister took her photograph. She seemed to be looking intelligently and inquiringly at it, but in reality I don't think she cared in the least about it.

These horned toads are really lizards, and in California we used to keep them in our rooms. Their most remarkable habit is that of ejecting blood from their eyes. My sister once saw a toad that was being teased spurt blood from its eyes. After exercising this power the toad often becomes limp and exhausted.

The Mexicans call them "sacred toads," because they weep these tears of blood. It is thought that this discharge of blood is a means of protection. When worried by a superior animal, the little toad can partly blind his enemy by shooting blood in his eye; and while the enemy is recovering from the pain, which the blood seems to cause him, the toad can make his escape.

The creature was not afraid of Sukey, and I never saw him shoot blood from his eyes while with us. Unfortunately he was stepped on and died.

Before Sukey was a year old she had a trying illness, brought on by a too rich diet and too much dancing.

One of my brothers had been with us for the Christmas holidays, and had brought his little girl with him. It amused us to see Sukey dance, so we used to blow lightly on her feet, and she would spin round and round for us. After a while her feet became purple and inflamed, and she went lame.

I put her in a basket, covered her up carefully, and took her to our kind family physician. He gave me an antiseptic wash, helped me bathe her claws and tie them up, for by this time they were very sore, and had turned black.

Sukey took this affliction so much to heart that she moped and would not eat. I had no intention of losing her, so I made pills of seeds and rolled oats and slipped them down her throat. In a short time she got well, but unfortunately lost two of the claws on one of her red feet. I cut short her supply of hemp seeds, for I had been too indulgent in the past. It is strange what a passion almost every bird has for this oily, rich seed. Even birds too small to crack it will eat voraciously of it when it is crushed.

CHAPTER XV

PIGEONS AND HAWKS

As Sukey grew older her indifference to other birds became stronger. I never saw her watch a bird or follow its motions with any interest, unless it was to get out of the way of a larger bird that she was afraid of, or to aim a blow at a little one that came too near her. She had identified herself with human beings; and if there were none near her, she drew her head into her hood and sat meditatively waiting for one to come along and play with her.

As she felt so keenly on the subject, I only allowed her to pay flying visits to the downstairs aviary. All winter, when she could no longer go out on the veranda, she trotted about the room I had given her, or sat buried in meditation on a box high up on the wall. That was her room, her big bed, her box, her pincushion, and her sunny window. She had driven me from it, though at first I had been willing enough to share it with her. She used to sleep at my feet, but when she developed an amusing but tiresome habit of waking up every morning at daylight, trotting up to the head of the bed and ordering me to play with her, I chose another room. She often visited me there, and when I was confined to my room by a cold, she always spent the day with me along with my books and newspapers. When my tray came up she was always excited and interested, and trotting up to it, examined it carefully. She particularly liked creamed toast and my little dish of butter.

One day I heard an outcry in the dining-room below, and found that she was being driven from the family butter plate there. When I hurried downstairs in the morning, fearful of being late at family devotions, I would often hear her coming after me, step by step, her little claws sounding plainly as she hopped, not flew down. She never used to fly unless obliged to do so to catch up with us. We did not fly, and identified with us as she was, she preferred our means of locomotion. While prayers were going on she sat demurely on a sofa back, occasionally murmuring "Rookety cahoo!" After breakfast she flew to my shoulder and descended with me to the aviary, strutted over the earth floor, then followed me upstairs to her room.

My study was also a favorite place, and often as I sat writing I would hear a light footstep, then a rush of wings, and Sukey was on my shoulder. After writing awhile I would look up at her and ask, "Do you approve of that sentiment, Sukey?" She always bowed her head politely, and this pigeon habit of bobbing the head was a great source of amusement to the neighbors' children, who often called on her.

"Are you glad to see the children, Sukey?" I would ask her, and her bow was always received with outbursts of laughter. Naturally I was careful only to ask questions that required an answer in the affirmative. If I became too much absorbed in my writing to play with her, she would get impatient, and descending to the desk, would catch at my pen or, naughtiest trick of all, drink from the ink bottle. Often I have looked up, discovered a dripping black beak, and have rushed from the room to wash her mouth.

Although she loved my study when I was alone, she hated it when it was full of company. Often visitors would beg to see the Princess, and I would send upstairs for her. She was not really afraid, but she hated a crowd, and after holding her by force a few minutes, I would put her on the floor, and with her ruff shaking with anger she would trot into the hall and go upstairs to her room.

One day she laid an egg on my writing-desk. I took it upstairs, made a nest of soft cloths for her, and put the egg in it. The third day she laid another egg. I advised her to take the bed for a nesting-place, and although she subsequently laid eggs in other places, this, for a long time, was her chosen home, and she would drive any other bird from its sacred precincts.

She seemed fascinated by these two eggs, and sat on them nearly all the time, caressing them, and turning them over and over with her beak. I was amused with her actions, for she had no shyness and no fear of human beings. Of course, every bird turns her eggs over to keep them in condition, but how seldom one sees a bird in the act of turning them. Sukey's actions with her eggs then and since convince me that she really had some kind of attachment for them. I had had an idea before this that the sitting on eggs was duty work, the only real pleasure coming with the nestlings.

If any bird dared alight near these precious eggs she would peck furiously at it. She was also reluctant to leave the eggs unless I would watch them. If I would sit down beside them she would at once step carefully off them, lift up her feet like a skirt dancer, and stretch first one long wing and then another, as if tired of sitting, then go for a walk about the room.

The instant I rose she would rush back to her nest, and if she got hungry before I had leisure to return to her, she would hurry to her seed-box and eat so rapidly that it seemed as if she would choke. She had made up her pigeon mind that she would not let those beloved eggs get cold.

Often as I sat by her nest she would bring me little wisps of straw, and would tuck them around the eggs, or would hold them out to me in her beak, meaning that I was to have the privilege of arranging them. Her actions were very curious and interesting, and I could not help wondering whether human beings were often honored by birds to the extent of being requested to assist in the work of making a nest.

Better than straws were hairpins, hatpins, or safety-pins.

She had been brought up in a bedroom, and my pincushion had always been an object of interest to her. I have seen her take a long hatpin in her beak, toss it up in the air, catch it, and go to her nest with it.

The invisible hairpins were her chief favorites, and one day my sister said to me, "I cannot imagine where all my invisible hairpins are."

"Go to Sukey's nest," I said, and there she found neatly arranged around the eggs the missing hairpins. I have often taken sharp pins from her nest, in the fear that she might stick them into herself.

After a time I began to worry about her prolonged sitting. She had no mate to relieve her, and to sit day and night, except in the short intervals when I took care of her eggs for her, was too great a strain on her constitution. So one day I went down to the aviary, got a youthful squab from one of the pigeon nests there, and taking away one of Sukey's eggs, slipped the squab in its place. Her back was turned to me during this last maneuver, but presently she came trotting along with a straw in her beak.

When she saw the squab she stopped short with a dreadful stare, then dropping her straw she took squabbie by the neck and shook his tender flesh till I hastened to rescue him, and gave her back her egg.

Later on I took her eggs away from her and put them in a covered box. She seemed to know they were in the box, for one day I found her trying to worry the cover off, and a second day she had the cover off and was sitting on the eggs. A third time I found her standing on the box and fighting my doves away from it. This time I turned the doves away, lifted the cover, and she stepped in and sat on the eggs. One day, after I had put the eggs in the box, she flew to my shoulder, and I felt something tickling my ear. Looking around I saw that she had a straw in her beak and was trying to coax me to put it beside the eggs.

I have often felt sorry that I have not kept a record of the number of eggs that my Princess has laid. She begins in the spring and lays all summer, sometimes one, sometimes two eggs, and at intervals of about six weeks. When she was two years old I took her with my other pigeons to my farm in the country.

I now had quite a number of pigeons. Among them a special favorite was Crippie, a lame black tumbler. He was fat and in good condition, but had had since he began life an absurd walk or waddle, his legs being spread very far apart. I had been advised to kill him, but had refused. There was nothing the matter with him but his lameness, and he was a dear, gentle bird, and had been partly brought up by hand. A tumbler is supposed to turn over and over in the air as he flies, but Crippie never tumbled.

Two other pet birds were homers—Tweedledum and Tweedledee. Their parents had deserted them, and they too had been brought up by hand. Then I had magpie pigeons, an exquisite white owl pigeon called Owlie, some archangels, and specimens of a few other birds.

I had had a demure nun pigeon that I bought in Boston. At least she looked demure with her convent-like garb, but she turned out to be a vixen, and used to drive my guineapigs about the aviary till they succumbed with fright. At first it was amusing to see her marshaling the pigs and driving them before her, but I soon found out that what was fun for her was death for the pigs, so I sent her away. When I took all these fancy pigeons to the country I confined them in a loft for a time till they got used to their new quarters and began to make nests. Then I opened a window and allowed them to go out.

My whole family was impressed by the delight of these birds in real, untrammeled liberty. For generations their ancestors had been kept in confinement, but there was enough wild blood left to make them appreciate what was now spread before them. The first day I let them out they flew about uncertainly, then sat in a row on top of the carriage-house. The building was reasonably high, the barn was higher, the near-by house was surrounded by tall trees, below them were meadows, plowed fields, and a pine wood. They had altogether two hundred acres of their own property, and beyond stretched one large farm after another, along one of the most beautiful valleys in the world—the one which finally reaches the far-famed land of Longfellow's "Evangeline."

No wonder that the pigeons were delighted. They timidly tried another flight, then another, wheeling in wider and wider circles, always coming back to the carriage-house, and gazing about them as if they were "lost in wonder, love, and praise," my father sagely remarked.

As the days went by they flew constantly about the farm. I never saw one leave it, though I heard of some of my old homers calling at distant farms. The young homers hatched on the place would, of course, not leave us.

Away beyond the farm was the long North Mountain, and beyond the mountain was the Bay of Fundy, well known for its high tides. So, in connection with my pigeons, I could truthfully recite Walter Prichard Eaton's lines:

The doorway of their coop unloosed, they spring
Straight up above the housetops noisily;
An instant pause, a sudden swoop of glee,
Then high against the blue on tireless wing
Their wide-expanding, perfect circles fling;
From that great height they look to open sea,
The far green woods smile up invitingly—
But still the keeper counts their homecoming.

Unfortunately, when we first went to the farm, there were a few hawks about that succeeded in carrying off a number of my beautiful pigeons. These hawks came with such frightful celerity that unless one sat all the time with a gun in hand it was impossible to shoot them. We could protect the chickens, for when the hawk was coming, the little wild birds that were fed about the farmhouse would scurry through the air in a hurried, unnatural way. If we noticed them, and called to the chickens, the petted things would run for shelter. Not so the pigeons. They never hurried to their lofts. When they saw a hawk they rose swiftly in the air and flew madly round and round.

The hawk would get the poor flyers, and any that were handicapped, except Crippie and Owlie. He never got them, and I wondered at it. He carried off a fine, red jacobin that I had sent up from Halifax, hoping Sukey would be friendly with him. She beat him so persistently that I put him out with the others. He looked very handsome sitting up aloft with his red hood about his head, but one day he disappeared, and later I found a heap of his pretty feathers at the foot of a pine tree where the hawk had carried him to tear him to pieces.

I lost twenty pigeons, but only three chickens. It was very pathetic to see those three disappearing. On one occasion I was close by. The hawk seemed to fall like a bullet from a clear sky. He seized the poor little unfortunate and bore it off by the head, its legs dangling helplessly in the air.

These hawks were not large ones, and at a little distance looked like one of my big homers. After a time we were not so much troubled by them. I had tried to get rid of them by keeping guineahens, for the country people round about said that no hawk will approach a farm where a guineahen is kept. I thought I would try the experiment, and bought a fine pair of guineahens that never wandered, as many of the tribe do. The hawks did not mind them at all, and swooped down on the chickens when they were close by.

Our best friends were the crows and the kingbirds. A pair of crows built a nest in a tall tree close to the boundary of our farm, and one of them was always sailing through the air to keep the hawks away. More intrepid than the crows were the kingbirds or beemartins, so called because of their supposed fondness for the honey bee, though it is now asserted that they eat only the drones. These kingbirds had a nest close to us, and it was most gratifying to see the way in which they chased both crows and hawks. They were better than a gun, and I used to wish long and earnestly that there was some way in which I could reward them.

CHAPTER XVI

SUKEY AND HER FOSTER-PIGEON

The winter after Sukey went up to the farm I had some anxiety about her. She had a poor digestion; she always was a small eater, and she seemed to feel the cold of the unusually severe winter we had. Every bitter night she had a copper foot-warmer to sit on, and I would often get up before daylight and give her something to eat. One peculiarity that she has is that she eats by artificial light, a thing that most pigeons will not do. She has always been accustomed to an eleven o'clock supper. She goes to bed at dark, but at eleven, when I enter the room with a lamp, she wakes up, stretches herself, greets me with an amiable "rookety cahoo!" then lets me lift her down to her seed-box, where she eats with the lamp close to her, runs her pink tongue over her lump of rock-salt, drinks heartily, and goes back to her perch.

I do not recommend this supper, except in the case of very delicate or sick birds. Sukey has been so frail that I have often found her almost dead from exhaustion, and she will not eat the different grains that other pigeons eat. She confines herself to rice, millet, and hemp.

When spring came she was much stronger, and I played an amusing trick on her. When she made a nest and laid eggs I went one day to the pigeon-loft outside, where my pet Tweedledum, a daughter of the bird that had come from England, had a nest. I pushed Tweedledum aside, saw that one of her eggs had just broken and a squab lay inside. I took the squab inside his egg-shell and went back to the house. Concealing what I carried I went up to Sukey and told her to go for a walk. This she was very happy to do, and while she was gone I took one of her warm eggs from the nest and put the young squab and his shell inside. Soon she returned, stopped short, and stared at the nest as if to say, "Is it possible that an egg of mine has hatched out at last?"

Then, as if her suspicions were aroused, she turned to me with a dreadful stare of inquiry. I did not dare to laugh. It seems to me that she has grown so intelligent that she knows when I am laughing at her. I nodded my head as if to say, "Yes, it is your own pidgie," then I pushed her on the nest.

She stepped very carefully over the little bird—it is wonderful to see the pains a mother bird takes not to injure little ones—she settled down over it. It was adopted. I was delighted. Now I would see what kind of a mother she would make. She sat on it steadily day after day, but to my amusement, for I had not reckoned on this, she started to feed it whole seeds from her crop.

She knew how to take its little beak in her own, this pigeon that had never associated with her kind; but of course she would have killed it with her whole seeds, so, as a punishment for the trick I had played on her, I had the task of feeding Sukey before she fed the squab. This I did by slipping pills of bread and rolled oats down her throat. To my further amusement the role of motherhood soon bored her. She did not really love birds, and she got tired of this squab as soon as he left the nest.

She is a slight creature, and this stout young homer with his big flapping wings, and his hoarse and piercing cries for food worried her and upset her usual calm. She ran from him, and we were often convulsed with laughter at the sight of Sukey fleeing from her adopted baby. I always had to catch him and feed him, and then he would go and squat down beside her and behave himself.

We called him Whistler, from his shrill cries after Sukey, and after a few weeks I again visited Tweedledum's nest and took out of it the squab I had left. I wanted to compare it with

Whistler, to see the difference between the one I had brought up and the one the mother had raised.

I found that mine was slightly smaller than hers, but was much more mature—it had a wiser eye, and acted more like a grown-up bird. Hers was more fluffy and was, of course, very shy. It snapped its bill at us and kept in a corner. Sukey began to beat it, so I hurried it back to Tweedledum.

When Whistler grew older he made his way out to the front and side of the house, where we had hammocks and tables, and always afternoon tea. Sukey, of course, came with him, and it was amusing to see these two birds perched on the hammock ropes while the four dogs lay underneath and the family sat about, reading and talking. In the distance were cats, hens, pigeons, sparrows, wild birds, calves, and pigs wandering about the farmyard and orchard.

If we all went into the house or disappeared about the farm, Sukey and Whistler would either follow us, or would go to the doors and wait for some one to let them in. I have often smiled to see baby Whistler all alone—such a tiny pigeon—standing patiently by the big hall door. Sukey would trot after us away down to the river, but he did not care as much for walking as she did.

They were never supposed to be left a minute alone out of doors, on account of the hawks, but sometimes we forgot them. One day we had been interested in the packing of some fine Siberian crabapples from a tree down by the road. All the family, including Sukey, had been there. When the dinner-bell rang we came back to the house, and not until we were at the table did I remember Sukey. I sprang up and rushed to the crabapple tree. She was not there. She had been sitting on a post, an easy mark for a keen-eyed hawk.

I ran back to the house, intending to ask the family to join me in a search for our especial pet, but it was not necessary. There, on the kitchen veranda, sat the little hooded creature patiently waiting for the door to be opened. After we left her she had trotted up the short avenue after us, and had taken her station there.

"Sukey," I said, as I caught her up, "I was afraid that the hawks had caught you."

"Oh, rookety cahoo!" she replied consolingly, "rookety cahoo!"

When I sold my farm and went back to the city I could not make up my mind to take the homers with me. They had enjoyed themselves so hugely in the country that I resolved to leave them. City life would mean confinement; for these farm-hatched birds, if let loose in Halifax, would endeavor to return to the farm.

I took only four pigeons back with me, Sukey, Whistler, Crippie, and Owlie. Poor Owlie died of some mysterious disease, and Crippie in his black tumbler suit, seems to mourn constantly and sincerely for her.

Whistler, I am sorry to say, after his return to the city, developed into a confirmed pugilist, and some one had to take time to fight with him every day. Bracing his two red feet firmly he would close his eyes, grunt vigorously, keep a tight hold on the finger that had been extended to him, and jerk convulsively like a dog that has hold of another dog's throat. His pinches and twists were so scientific that at last we wore gloves while contesting with him. After getting pretty well warmed up he would vary the twisting process by giving hard slaps with his wings.

Two years ago I was going away from home for a few months, and begged my father to have the care of entertaining Whistler, for his beatings were too severe for my mother. My father obligingly consented, and every day while I was gone put on a pair of gloves and went into the aviary to let Whistler fight him.

The bird, at this time, used to sit the most of the time by

the aviary door, waiting for us to come and amuse him. His upbringing with Sukey had unfitted him for pigeon society, and if he had not been so rough I would have allowed him to come upstairs with her.

She was shocked and disgusted by his bullying ways, and would have nothing to do with him. He deteriorated until he became dangerous, and one day this last summer when I went into the aviary I taxed him with the disappearance of Crippie, my beloved lame tumbler.

He, of course, gave me no satisfaction, and after a time I discovered my poor cripple creeping from under a tree with a battered and bleeding head, and one eye closed. I washed and dressed his wounds, and took Whistler upstairs to my room. "You are a very bad bird," I said, "I don't know what I am going to do with you." He strutted and cooed and gurgled with glee, and walked round and round me. This was just what he wanted—to come upstairs with me.

"Go into that closet, you wicked pigeon," I went on, "and sleep there." This was still better fun. He walked into the closet, found some rubbers there, and began to talk to them. "At last you have some safe playmates," I went on, "you may beat them as much as you like."

There were two storm rubbers and two sandals, and as the days went by I saw that Whistler really considered them some new kind of pigeons. He bowed politely to them, pushed them about with his beak, talked to them, and one day I took an egg of Sukey's, made a nest, and put it in the closet with a sandal on top of it. Then I called Whistler, who looked delighted with this new arrangement. He gave an agreeable nod to the sandal, gently moved it aside with his beak, and stepping on the nest, sat all night beside the egg.

Of course I did not keep him in the closet all the time. He spent a good deal of time with me, in no danger of being trodden on, for I have been so much with birds that I have developed a shuffling gait in order to avoid stepping on them.

Every morning I put him out on the roof-veranda, but he was never allowed to be alone with Sukey. If I left him I got some other member of the family to watch him. He behaved himself as long as we were present, but if left alone with her would seize her by the long neck feathers and wipe the floor with her. Sukey, who had continued developing, was now far beyond him. She abhorred this barbaric conduct, and more than ever before fled from him in terror.

She had now gone in for scientific nest-making, and her materials were more and more peculiar. One of the last I pulled to pieces consisted of assorted sizes of hairpins, a black-headed pin, a half-burnt match, a withered mayflower, a feather from an indigo bunting's wing, and some little sticks of different shapes. I saw her one day tossing my mother's spectacles up in the air, as if deliberating whether to put them in the nest or not. Finally she threw them on the floor.

Another thing that she did not throw on the floor, but put in the nest, was a garnet finger-ring that she stole from my dressing-table. I took it out, but it soon afterward disappeared. However, if Sukey lost it she did it unintentionally, for the nest would be its destination.

In addition to varying the materials she chose different and safer places for her nests. An old fur cloak, folded up on the telephone-table is a favorite spot. Last summer she sat there a great deal of the time, and did not object strongly to any member of the family using the telephone, but growled ominously when a stranger approached. One day I heard a man plead with her not to grumble at him.

Always of a jealous disposition, she has become more sensitive as to any attention bestowed on other birds. She will leave her food at any time to fly to me, and protest vigorously if she hears me petting another bird. If I am feeding a young one she flies right on it, jabbering excitedly, and tries to wean my attention from it to herself. She does not like us to notice any other creature, and some time ago she gave an exhibition of what we thought was jealousy of a dog.

She had been sitting on two eggs, and my mother one day took them from her. Sukey eyed her strangely as she did so, for to have any person but myself take her eggs was an exceptional thing. After my mother left the room Sukey followed her, and I followed Sukey. My mother had disappeared, but Sukey pressed right on to her bedroom, and flew to the arm of a rocking-chair. There she sat gazing pensively at my mother's little dog Billy, who lay in a chair by the bed.

"What are you doing in here, Sukey?" I asked, "you never come in this room. Come back to your own."

I took her there, but she would not stay, and once again I followed her to my mother's room, where she sat staring at Billy.

I told the family of the occurrence, and we concluded that it was possible that Sukey had, in pigeon fashion, reasoned that my mother had stolen her eggs to put them under her own pet—the dog.

Sukey did not dare to beat him, although the dog always treated her with the greatest consideration. She never hesitates to beat birds smaller than herself if she gets angry with them or with me. Sometimes when I am reading or sewing she caresses me until she gets tired, then puts her head down for me to rub it. If I am too much absorbed to do so, she beats me. Then I push her from me. Her eyes sparkle, she goes round and round on the floor, saying angrily, "rookety cahoo!" then darts at the nearest bird, usually an unoffending white dove that loves to be near her. The little dove's feathers fly until I spring up, rescue her, pick the white down from Sukey's bill, and apologize for my inattention. In these fits of rage she reminds me of children who do not dare to strike their parents, and who attack some one smaller than themselves.

A curious trait in this pet pigeon of mine is her sensitiveness to any change in my dress. At first I could not believe that she distinguished colors, and knew an old gown from a new one, but at last I became fully convinced of it.

Pigeons wear the same gown all the time. They do not moult into different colors, and Sukey does not like me to do so. When I moult into a new hat or a new gown she is either in a fright or a rage. If the former, she holds herself erect, packs her feathers and becomes slim, and grunts like an Indian several times—"Ugh, ugh, ugh!"

One can never mistake the pigeon sound of fright. If she is merely angry she flies on the hat, bites it, scolds incessantly, and shows her displeasure with me by talking rapidly. In the case of a dress she trots round and round me on the floor, biting the hem in displeasure. I have been amused with the curious way in which she dissociates my hands from my head. Some time ago I found out that she considers my hands aliens and enemies. She loves my head, but when she is caressing it the unkind hands often lift her away. So she spends hours in fighting them, and sometimes as I sit reading with her on my lap, I have to hide my hands or she bites them till they are sore.

CHAPTER XVII

MINNIE POST-OFFICE

During the six years that I have had Sukey she has spent all her winters, except the one on the farm, in her warm, furnace-heated room upstairs. Last winter I became worried about her throat, and had our family doctor examine it and prescribe for her. He gave her tincture of iron, and for a long time she had her little bottle of medicine and her tiny spoon and dropper.

I had been in the habit of keeping a few other delicate birds upstairs with her, but finding that the inhabitants of the lower aviary did not get sore throats, nor very dried-up claws, I decided that Sukey had been kept too warm, and resolved to put her and all my other birds downstairs.

If I had been at home it would have been a very difficult matter to keep her there. However, I was coming away, and I could not bring her with me, so a week before I left I carried my pet bird down to the inhospitable room in which she had been thrown from her nest as a baby, and told her she must stay there.

She ran after me to the wire door and begged to come out. I told her that the imprisonment was for her good. Her health would probably improve, and she would become less abnormal. I had been educating her out of her sphere.

She is not the kind of bird to die of grief, but she did not like my plan for her. She placed herself on a stone ledge by the door and sat there night and day, except when eating and drinking. I fastened a little box against the wall for her to sit on, and left strict injunctions with the maid who was to take care of her that if she fretted she was to be taken upstairs.

She does not fret. She eats and drinks and sits on her box, but all the time she is listening for me. When she hears any one coming in the basement she calls out, hoping that I am returning.

She is receiving a great deal of petting from my parents, and the maid writes that occasionally my pet bird lights on her shoulder. However, I know that no one can take my place with my pigeon. She is as faithful as a dog, and bird-lovers will understand how eagerly I look forward to a reunion with her. It would be unwise to project into her the emotional qualities of a human being. She is not suffering, she is only waiting, but it is something to be able to wait in the days of a fickle and restless generation.

Poor Whistler too is waiting, but I cannot feel the same sympathy for him that I do for my Princess, and I smile whenever I think of him. He, for the winter, is alone in the cage that was built for my owl. It is a good size, and he is high-stepping round it and talking incessantly to a pigeon that I got in rather a curious way.

One day last summer one of the numerous boys who bring me birds, rang the bell, and announced that a new pet was approaching.

I tried not to laugh when I found that my new pet's carriage was a steam roller. The big, dirty, noisy thing was drawn up near the house. A man black as the roller, from his contact with the coal, was coming toward the door, and in his hand he held a sooty pigeon.

"It is from the post-office," he said; "I was taking the roller by, and frightened two pigeons so that they fell from their nest. One went among the market women, and I don't know what became of it. This fellow lighted on my box, and though the boys begged for it, I shut it up and brought it to you."

The post-office is about a mile from our house. I thanked him for his kindness to the bird, and invited him upstairs to see its new home. He followed me to the roof-veranda, and I examined the bird. One squawk that it gave, and its size, proclaimed it to be young, just ready to leave the nest.

"I will feed it for a day or two," I said, "then let it go."

He thanked me and went away, and I fed that pigeon from the last day of July till the last day of September.

"What is the matter with it?" I asked, "is it bewitched? Its capacity for food seems endless."

I never had fed a pigeon for so long a time, but Minnie Post-office, as we named her, did not seem able to get a morsel to stay in her bill.

If I did not feed her she would peck at seeds, but they rolled right out of her mouth. For several weeks my brother-in-law assisted me in feeding her, as I had a number of other birds that no one but myself could care for. Three times a day her dish of water, her box of pills, and her feeding bib were brought out. She was a wild pigeon, and in order to keep her still during meal-time we had to put a cloth around her shoulders.

When my brother-in-law had to return to his university, and October approached, I put Minnie downstairs in the aviary.

"I am very sorry," I said to her, "but I can feed you no longer. If you can't pick up food for yourself, you will have to starve or be poisoned."

I tried her for a few days. Her crop always seemed empty, but she lived; and, to my delight, Whistler struck up a friendship with her. I put a box close to the wire netting of his cage, and he stood on a box inside, and Minnie stood on the one outside, and they talked to each other all day long.

One day I put her inside his cage, but she was frightened, and he did not care half as much for the attainable as for the unattainable. When I separated them they went on billing and cooing, and I know are at it yet.

It is an excellent way for her to spend her time. Birds must have something to take up their attention or they mope to death. I know that my gentle Crippie stirs Sukey up occasionally and makes her trot about the ground enough to give her exercise.

One other pigeon I have in my aviary—the Tramp—that a little boy brought to me a week or two before I left home.

"I found this bird in a field," he said; "I guess his wing is broken."

The wing was not broken. I kept the bird by himself for some time, and decided that he was half-starved and deadly weary. He had started to moult, and his poor jagged feathers had not been able to carry him more than a few feet from the ground. I put him in with the others, and left him eating and drinking and meditating. I hope he will not put on flesh and beat his fellows before I return.

When I get on the subject of pigeons it is difficult for me to stop talking. I shall be pleased if I have convinced any doubters that they are really intelligent birds, and the ones most suitable for domestication. Any one can keep a few by giving them a room or a part of a room in an attic and allowing them to fly in and out through an open window.

One thing I am firmly convinced of—pigeons should always be under supervision. Bird-lovers are not apt to be annoyed by them, but non-bird-lovers often complain, and justly complain, of unwished-for birds that come and make untidy nests and disfigure their buildings. Every city should maintain pigeon-lofts. There should be, in a few exposed places, rooms where they can go in and lay eggs in boxes prepared for them. The cost would be trifling, and one would have the squabs to dispose of.

I have educated myself into laying sentiment aside. Pigeons should not be allowed to increase indefinitely, nor should large flocks be fed all summer and be allowed to starve all winter. They should be regulated. Every summer a certain number of squabs should be mercifully killed.

I managed in this way on my farm: Each pair of birds had two large nesting-boxes. When their first pair of squabs was ready to leave the nest they were just suitable for the market. I gently lifted them out and delivered them over to one of the men about the farm. The little creatures had had a happy life. They had an instantaneous death. The parents, taken up with the second nest, never resented the removal of the first pair of squabs. Whereas, if I had kept taking their eggs from them, they would have become uneasy, and would have tried to find a safe place to build.

It would have been cruel to keep all my squabs. Few farmers wanted them. I could not feed a large number, and I decided that the right way was to kill them, though that one thing—the necessity of taking life would easily have destroyed my pleasure in farm life, if I had allowed it to do so.

One thing I have discovered about them, making them more suitable than any other birds for pets, is that they do not mind careful handling. My pigeons climb about me like pups, and they are the only birds I have that do not object when a hand is laid over their wings. All my other tame birds will light on my shoulder or hand, allow me to talk to them, but would be overcome with uneasiness if I put my hand over their only means of escape from an enemy—their wings.

My pigeons go to sleep on my lap, and let me fondle them as much as I choose. Indeed, I should say from what I know of them, that a pigeon that has once formed an attachment for a human being, will never entirely go back to pigeon society.

CHAPTER XVIII

MY FIRST CANARIES

Some years ago I heard John Burroughs lecture in Boston in the rooms of the Procopeia Club on "Observation of Nature."

He said that we see in life what we look for, and told of Thoreau who had a great faculty for finding arrow-heads. A friend with whom he was walking one day asked him how he found them.

"In this way," replied Thoreau, stooping down and picking one up.

After I became interested in birds I found them all around me, and even in my small native city discovered that there existed several fine collections of birds, especially of canaries.

I visited these collections and, observing the great variety of canaries, found that it is with them as it is with pigeons. The original stock has been so transformed and improved on that one cannot recognize the little wild ancestral canary of the islands off the coast of Africa, in their diversified descendants.

There are the nervous, high-strung Belgian canaries with the humps on their backs, making them look like tiny yellow camels, the Scotch fancies with their half-circles of bodies, the insignificant looking Germans with their exquisite song, the fluffy French, the strangely marked hybrids, and the large, handsome English birds, often eight inches long and with brilliant coloring.

This coloring arises from the desire of bird-dealers to have scarlet birds. They used to have plenty of deep-gold canaries, and in order to intensify this color, tried experiments in feeding saffron, cochineal, port wine, and beet-root to no avail; but finally a bird-keeper discovered that cayenne pepper was what he needed to turn yellow to scarlet and make his birds the sensation of the canary world.

My first canaries were, however, none of these thoroughbreds. In those days I did not think of raising young ones, and one day taking pity on some underfed, ugly birds in the house of a poor woman, I bought two and took them home with me. They were not clean and they were not pretty. The sickly, yellow one I named Jessie, the dark-green one with a pitiful attempt at a crest I called Minnie. Jessie did not live long. She had no constitution, and one of my Brazil cardinals took a dislike to her and struck her, and though I rescued her, she finally died. To replace her I got another—this one a prettier bird called Jennie.

My next canary was a thoroughbred, the son of an English prize bird. I paid five dollars for him, which was very cheap. I fell in love with him, as he nervously danced about his cage, and as long as I had him he was the most remarked bird in my aviary. He was much larger than the ordinary canary. His body was mottled green and yellow, his heavy crest hung so thick and drooping over his eyes that it partially obscured his sight, and the long, silky feathers of his body and legs made him look as if he had petticoats on. He was really a monstrosity, but was such a dear bird and so interesting, and withal so intelligent, that all the members of the family loved him.

He was terribly intense. I never before and never since have seen a bird that took such a vivid, picturesque interest in everything that went on around him. I put him in my study when I got him, and, tossing his head so that he could look under his drooping crest, he examined everything in the room and every one that came into it. To my delight he soon began to sing—a heavy, overpowering song, and as he sang he danced like a professional dancer, shaking and twisting and agitating his long feathers.

When I got him it was winter-time, and I did not dare to put him in the aviary lest he should take cold. So, as he could not go down to Minnie and Jennie, I brought them up to him. They had a large cage near one of the windows, but not too close to it, for canaries do not like draughts any better than human beings do. They were supposed to stay in their cage, but they spent the most of their time out in the room with me.

Norwich, as I called my beauty, was enraptured with these new birds, and almost agitated himself to death in trying to make himself agreeable. Minnie was his favorite from the first, and Jennie fell into unhappy jealousy.

Minnie really had a most extraordinary amount of character and individuality for such a tiny bird. She was self-willed, determined, clever, and full of resources. She made up her mind that Norwich should like her better than he did Jennie, and she swayed him to her will. He was good-natured, agreeable, and anxious to please—a mere tool in the hands of such a clever bird as Minnie. When Minnie had, by various wiles and devices, succeeded in attaching him to herself, she began to think of nest-making.

I cared nothing about raising young birds, and gave them only an amused attention. She flew all about my study, picked every floating bit of down and shining motes from the floor, seized feathers and scraps of paper, and chose as her first nesting-place—one of the gas globes. As fast as she placed a bit of nesting material in the globe, it fell to the floor. This did not discourage her for a long time, for the patience of birds is infinite. They work steadily and persistently at anything they wish to accomplish, and seem to think with the great Napoleon, that a difficulty is merely something to be overcome. They are also sweet-tempered, and not at all resentful toward any person or any bird who might help them in accomplishing their object, whatever it happens to be, but who does not do so.

So Minnie worked steadily on day after day until, at last, she was convinced that the globe was certainly bottomless, and I was convinced that I was acting very shabbily in not encouraging so industrious and patient a bird. I therefore fashioned a rough nest out of twigs—for I was new to the business myself—and put it in a corner of her cage.

She watched me with great interest and curiosity, and as soon as I had left the cage, flew to it, examined it, and adopted it as her own. It was a shaky structure, but the little uncomplaining bird found it quite satisfactory, and was delighted to discover that the pieces of cloth and string she put in did not fall through the bottom of it.

This was not my first experience with the curiosity of birds; I had found that I could not enter the aviary and throw down even a scrap of paper without having a cloud of birds around it as soon as my back was turned, picking at it, pulling it, as if to discover why I had put it there.

Birds and animals know more than we think they do, and they certainly have some way of reading our minds, probably by some slight visible sign.

When my father in his study forms the design of going downtown, the dog at his feet rises, and shows by his actions that he knows of this design. What tells him? My father has done nothing to acquaint the dog with his purpose just formed.

Apparently he has done nothing, yet he has. He has put by his pen with an air of finality, or he has pushed back his chair in a certain way, or he has glanced at his watch. Something tells the little, intelligent creature, who guesses the meaning of my father's action more quickly than we human beings would, that he is going out of the house.

In the same way, I have been struck by the certainty that when I enter the aviary with the intention of catching a certain bird, he knows it, and he alone gets excited. If my sister were with me she would not know which bird I was about to lay my hands on. The particular bird knows by the glance I give him.

When Minnie had finished lining the nest I gave her, and

began to sit on it, Jennie became wild with jealousy. She flew at the nest, pulled pieces from it, and was such a scandal and shame to Minnie and Norwich that, wishing to please her too, I made another nest and put it in the other end of the cage.

Now she too was happy, and began to lay eggs and to sit on them. I thought this a satisfactory condition of affairs, but as time went on I became convinced that two hen canaries should not have nests in the same cage.

Norwich spent all his time with Minnie. He sat by her, talked to her, filled his beak with food that he put in her pleading one, and sang to her, until the exasperated Jennie would call out as if to say, "Have you not a word for me?"

Norwich would draw himself up, look at her uneasily, as if he were asking, "Why can't you let a fellow alone?" then would continue his attentions to Minnie.

Jennie almost boiled over, and leaving her nest flew at Minnie's, often seizing a beakful of stuffing, to the great detriment of the eggs. Minnie too had a temper, and lowering her head and spreading her wings, would rush at her former friend, shaking like a little fury, while the uneasy Norwich would almost fidget himself off his claws, squeaking uncomfortably as if to say, "I don't see why you two ladies can't agree!"

I soon took Jennie away. She was a nice little bird, and I did not like to see her unhappy. She went back to the aviary, and lived there happily for some time.

Now ensued a season of calm for Minnie and Norwich. In thirteen days her eggs began to hatch. I had never seen young canaries before, and examined them with deep interest as they lay at the bottom of the nest—three tiny yellow and red lumps of flesh, developing long necks and microscopic open beaks when Norwich touched them tenderly with his own.

How he did stuff them! I wish that all human babies had such devoted parental affection as those tiny birds had. All day long he hung over them, and the instant the little heads were raised he was ready with his beak full of the perfectly fresh egg-food I made for them.

Every night he nestled close beside them and Minnie. I have never had another canary do this, the father bird usually sleeping a little way from the mother. Norwich and Minnie were a remarkable pair. She was so businesslike and resourceful; he was so intensely sensitive and affectionate.

The young birds developed wonderfully, and in three weeks were as large as their parents, and had hopped out of the nest. Fortunately, these were fine, large birds, more like the handsome father than the dowdy mother, but as time went by I saw the importance of careful selection in the mating of birds. I had and have children and grandchildren, great-grandchildren and great-great-grandchildren of my handsome Norwich and underbred Minnie. Many of these birds are strong, and nervous, and handsome like the father. Several of them have been subject to mysterious decline and death. There the poor blood on the mother's side of the house comes in. Have good parents and you have good offspring.

As soon as the warm weather came I put Norwich and Minnie out on the roof-veranda. Now they were happy, and disproved all the nonsense that is talked about caged birds preferring a cage to liberty. I grant that a canary always has a certain lack of fear with regard to a cage. He will enter it to feed, even to sleep, but if you leave the door open he will spend more time outside of it than in it.

Any of my canaries would fly about the street outside our house and would return to the roof-veranda. I have no doubt but what I could have allowed many of them this liberty all the time if it had not been for the cats. These cats were most amusing. I am fond of the cat tribe, and could not find it in my heart to be angry with them, for they were so perfectly open and frank in their demands for birds.

One old fellow would follow me about the garden as I looked for green stuff for the birds. His mouth was wide open, he was fairly yelling for a nice plump pigeon or canary, or a bright-headed foreigner.

"Pussy, it is quite impossible," I would say gravely; "I love those birds, I cannot give them to you to crunch to pieces in your jaws."

"Me-ow, wow!" he would cry in despair, and would go and sit close to the aviary windows and watch them.

The birds did not mind him, nor the other half-dozen felines that gazed with him. They only minded the nocturnal ventures of the cats, for there were enterprising ones that climbed the twenty feet into the air of the wire elevator and promenaded over the roof of the second story of the house. Often at night I have been awakened by a cry of distress from a bird or a sound of wings beating against the wire netting and, stealing out, have found an adventurous pussy on the roof. These cats never went down the way they came up. Every few mornings I had the task of inducing my cat friends to return to terra firma.

One day I was amused to see a neighbor's child with a lone kitten in his hands, begging an old cat to come down off the roof to her young one. She did not, till I assisted her—this time, I think, by means of a bean-pole. Finally, a cat got up on the roof, and would not come down. No kind of persuasion touched her. So I sent for a carpenter and a ladder, and after he brought pussy down I had him put a wide board round the elevator that said, "so far and no farther," to the cats.

To return to Norwich and his first nest of baby birds, and also his subsequent ones. I think I allowed him and Minnie to raise three sets of young ones this first summer, though two would have been enough, so great a strain on the mother is the rearing of nestlings.

I wanted to know whether the father bird taught the babies to sing. I used to watch these young ones when they began to listen to the singing around them, and made first faint, hoarse efforts at song themselves. Norwich too listened to them with evident pleasure, and sang a great deal himself, in a way that showed the act of singing was a relief to his nervous, excitable nature. He was apparently not trying to teach them. He sang when angry or glad—he wanted to express his own emotion.

I never saw him or any other father bird deliberately try to give the young ones a lesson. The young ones certainly acquired something from the father's song, but they also took up the notes of other birds. No two birds sang alike. There was always a slight variation.

As time went by and I got other canaries, there was a great deal of quarreling. Canary fights consist of shrieks and screams of anger, a flying together high up in the air, with a great fluttering of wings and striking of beaks, then a coming down again. It is all fuss and feathers with no bloodletting.

Norwich, with his long feathering, was perfectly ludicrous when he quarreled. He would tremble with rage, and from under his crest which, by the way, I had shortened when he went into the aviary, he would dart furious glances at any canary that happened to be meddling with him. Then, when his rage was over, or not quite over, he would dance and sing as if his little throat would burst.

CHAPTER XIX

RAISING YOUNG BIRDS

My canaries with their bites, and nips, and blows, reminded me of naughty children. However, it does not do for a bird to be too meek in an aviary. The bird that, when struck on one cheek, turns another, must say good-bye to happiness. The bird that keeps out of the way and is never attacked, gets on very well, but the bird that is not afraid to stand up to a bully, has the best time of all.

I was amused with a hen bird one day that was attacked by a larger bird. She had no time to fly, but she opened her beak and spread her wings, and made such a horrible and such a determined face that her assailant yielded her the perch and flew away.

I saw many singing contests, especially when there were two males anxious to please one female. The first canary would do his prettiest, then would deliberately stop and listen to his rival. I have often seen this first canary hitch up to his rival, and peer down his distended throat as if to say, "Where does all that noise come from?"

My canaries were the most industrious birds I had. I have never yet had a canary in health, that when spring began, was not immediately seized with a rage for nest-making that lasted till late in the autumn.

They like a new nest for every clutch of eggs, and a canary whose ancestors have been kept in cages for generations, will go right back to his wild habit of building in trees if you do not give him a nest-box. Even if there is a nest-box, some prefer the trees. I used a great many traveling-cages for nests, and hung them on trees and walls where the little birds could find them and build inside. These tiny cages, made of fir, whittled during the long winter evenings in Germany by miners and woodcutters, and sold for two and a half cents a cage, were for the canaries what the cracker boxes were for the pigeons. They were protected at the backs and sides, and the father birds could sit on the top. From the fronts of the cages I removed a few bars so the parents could go in and out.

It was wonderful to see the little canaries at work, flying to and fro with their beaks full of nesting materials. Fibrous roots should be given them, long, fine dry grass, cow or dog hair, rabbit down and feathers, though my canaries got enough of the latter in the aviary. Cotton wool and long lengths of twine should not be provided lest they entangle their feet.

When I found that my canaries liked soft white string better than anything else, I cut it in short bits for them. They discarded any bright-colored material, except for the interior of the nest, and I supposed this was because they did not wish to attract attention. It was amusing to see two birds tugging at one piece of twine, neither not in the least inclined to yield. The hen canaries used to shriek and scream at each other, and then their mates would interfere, and there would be a general fight.

In addition to singing when angry, birds sing when sad. One sunny day last March, when I let my birds out in the elevator, one bird sang so exquisitely that I could not help saying to myself, "Any one going by this house would say, 'What a happy bird!'—whereas I know he is singing because his little heart is nearly breaking." I had just found his mate dead in the aviary. She was a bird I had only had for a short time, and I think was very delicate. She never got to know me well, and was not fond of me, and when she for several days detached herself from other birds, and came about me, I was afraid I was going to lose her.

I have noticed again and again, without exactly

understanding it, that an ailing bird that is doomed, will follow me about and watch me, as if seeking the help I cannot give. Any bird is tamer when sick than when well. A beautiful bullfinch, that I once had, became so tame before he died that he would go to any member of the family. One day my mother called me and, pointing to this pretty creature in his shining hood of black and his crimson breast, she said, "Who is this little negro? He is sitting on my comb, and he just now dipped his beak in that mug. What does he want?"

"He is ill," I said, "and thirsty, and I am going to lose him," and I filled the mug with water, whereupon he drank with evident pleasure.

To come back to the matter of birds singing from unhappiness. I have had persons say to me, "My canary is perfectly happy, he sings all the time."

If it is the springtime, I say, "I am sorry for your bird; he is lonely. Why do you not give him a large cage and get another canary to be company for him? He might not sing so much, but he would be happier."

"Oh, I don't want a large cage—it would be in the way. I think he is all right."

Later on birdie often dies, and my friend buys another.

The traffic in canaries is simply enormous. In Germany, France, England, and Belgium, bird-keepers are hard at work raising young canaries for the American trade. American bird-importing houses employ a large number of men who go from one breeding-house to another in Europe and select the birds to be brought to New York, which is the distributing depot for the United States and Canada.

If the little bird singing in your window is insignificant in appearance, but has an exquisite song, he probably came from the Hartz Mountains. Very likely the principal income of the inhabitants of the village in which he was hatched, is derived from canary-raising.

They have bird schoolrooms with a school-teacher's box in which will be found an old bird, trained by a lark or a nightingale. When the time comes the cover is raised from the teacher's box. As he sees the light he bursts into a sweet, beautiful song, in long, low trills, deep rolls, flutes, turns, bells, bubbles, and other exquisite technicalities. The young birds stop feeding to listen, and in time, they too become perfect. The Germans educate their birds as thoroughly as they do their human singers, and they command excellent prices for them.

When the little birds are fully trained, some of the best are kept at home, and the others come in immense and valuable shipments to America in the tiny wicker cages. There is often great suffering among them. The voyage may be rough or disease may break out. The bird-dealers are said to do all they can to protect them, and only send experienced men with them, but the birds have many enemies, notably rats. Their attendants must watch day and night to protect their tiny charges.

It seems as if there might be American schools for canaries, if they must still be sold for cage-birds. A bird hates travel, and one shudders to think of the sufferings of our little feathered friends on the long journeys.

One day I found in Halifax one of these little German birds. He had just come from New York, and I bought him, took him home, and called him St. Andreasberg and Andy for a nickname. His only blemish was a pair of very scaly legs. That meant either old age or disease. However, they soon improved, though he has never had really smooth legs and claws.

He was a tiny fellow, pale yellow with a suspicion of black over one eye. He was not a first-class singer, but he had long, rippling notes, and when I heard him sing for the first time I was enraptured. I had never heard a lark sing, nor a nightingale. Andy's notes gave me some idea of what their song would be, for he was evidently a trained singer.

I got another little German bird for him, and the two have been model parents, raising one set of young Germans after another, until now I have their descendants to the third and fourth generations. They don't all sing as well as he does. If I had shut them up in a room with him, they might have done so, but I let them all go in the aviary, and mixing with Norwich's family, they soon learned to sing partly in the English way.

It is very amusing to hear one of these German birds begin his father's strain then break off and sing in Norwich's style. Only one German bird—Andy's first young one—sings almost the same song that his father does.

I am delighted with the flight of these birds—the offspring of caged birds. Norwich never learned to fly well. He had a kind of scalloping flight, but all his young ones fly like wild birds. Andy's are just as swift, and I find that these birds raised in an aviary are invariably stronger and larger than their parents. Greater variety of food and more exercise account for this.

Though I gave Norwich his liberty, I kept Andy in a cage for years. His eldest son hated him, and that brings me to one of the mysteries of bird life. The father and mother are devotion itself while bringing up a set of nestlings. They really seem to love the tiny creatures so dependent on them that they would perish if left to themselves. However, when the time comes for young birds to leave the nest or, rather, when the time comes for them to feed themselves—for most parents feed them for some days after they have stepped out, or have been pushed out of their home—the parents are either indifferent to them or are apparently cruel to their formerly beloved offspring. They fly away from them, they often push and beat them, they usually seem to have no affection for them. Andy fed his little son until he was old enough to feed himself, then he turned against him and did not want him in the big cage with him.

I thought this was quite natural, as Andy wished to make another nest, so I turned the young one into the aviary. He did not forget his father. Oh no, he remembered him only too well, and whether prompted by feelings of revenge or not, I cannot tell, but for years when he could elude me he would follow his father's cage and fight with him through the bars until he had plucked out all the short feathers about Andy's beak, and made the place raw and bleeding.

Of course I stopped this by keeping the cage out of his way, and I did not dare to let Andy loose in the aviary until about a year ago. Then I thought I would try the experiment. Andy had two dangers ahead of him. He was an old bird—he was old when I got him, and I had had him several years—and his son would certainly seek his life. However, I let him and his mate out on the roof-veranda. They got on beautifully, this pair of elderly birds. There was no affection for the cage in their tiny breasts. They forsook it, moped if I put them back in it, built nests as high up as birds that had never been in a cage, fought the son and came out even—a little exercise is good for a bird. I believe more caged winged creatures die from monotony than anything else—and they are to-day living happily in the aviary with big and little birds.

It is wonderful how aviary life preserves birds. Last summer there was a number of very fine English birds for sale in a store, and I watched one among them with interest for weeks. All his companions were sold, and he was left.

One day I said to the bird-dealer, "Give him to me to take home. He wants special attention and food."

"Take him," he said, "he is dying with asthma."

I took the bird home, named him the Britisher, and let him loose on the veranda, found he was frightened to death and could not fly, and put him in a large cage. For weeks he had egg-food, bread and milk, crushed hemp, plenty of green stuff, all kinds of seeds, in fact anything he wanted to eat. Then I once more opened his cage door. He sat about for a few days, then sallied forth, learned to fly, and stole a mate from another canary, one of my swift-flying, aviary-hatched birds; then with fearful recklessness he chose the most dangerous corner of the veranda for a nest, close to the spot my Brazil cardinals considered sacred to themselves. I don't know why they did not drive him away, or kill him. For days he sat complacently near them, guarding himself from the attacks of the swift flyer, whose mate he had stolen.

I put some food and water on a shelf near him, for if he descended on the floor he was at a disadvantage. Finally, I found him with a badly bitten leg, and put him back in his cage. His little mate followed him in, and stayed with him until he was able to go out again. He descended into the aviary with the other birds when the cold weather came, and it used to delight me to see the big, handsome, delicate creature sitting breathing spasmodically, but enjoying himself, watching his little mate.

He did not succumb till a week or two ago. When the maid wrote me that "a big yellow bird had died, and was bearried in the garden, it being a very hard thing to bearry it," I knew I had lost my bird of short, brief friendship—my pet Britisher.

Two of Andy's grandchildren, little beauties called Cowlie and Tippet, did a pretty thing last summer that seemed intentional. As the veranda is large, members of the family often sit out among the birds, and this pleases the tamest ones very much. They come sociably about us, perch on our laps or shoulders, peck at our work-baskets and try to run away with threads that we snatch from them. A favorite trick to play on the birds is to let them seize the end of the thread on a spool. Thinking they have a prize they fly away but soon find that their prize is endless and give it up in disgust.

Cowlie one evening, had been hanging about my sister

who was reading in the sunset. He was singing his prettiest good-night song, and he was so persistent about it that at last she dropped her book and began to praise him

He listened with his pretty yellow head on one side, then flew downstairs and came back with his young brother Tippet, who is as fine a singer as he is, and a remarkable little bird. When he was still a baby and being fed by his parents I have seen him fill his beak with the egg-food and feed other babies younger than himself.

Having brought Tippet to my sister, Cowlie began a duet with him, and until it was time for them to fly to their perch for the night, delighted us with an exquisite flow of rippling bird-music. I do not know a prettier sight than a little bird in full song. My young Germans often lift one claw as they sing and distend their little throats till we laugh at them, and tell them they look as if they were trying to raise tiny yellow beards.

One day I got one of these aviary-hatched young ones and put him in a cage. He was not frightened, but he was so puzzled at my action that he did not know what to do. What was the cage anyway, and what were the perches for? It never seemed to occur to him to light on them. He clung uncomfortably to the side of the cage till I at last took pity on him and let him fly out to the trees of the aviary.

The number of nests that the canaries made did not embarrass me, but what should I do with the eggs. I could not treat them as I did the pigeon eggs, and I was not willing to raise young birds and give to friends to put in tiny cages. I at last hit upon the expedient of visiting my canary nests every few days, and taking out a certain number of eggs till they were all gone. The canaries did not care much about eating them, but Dan, the mockingbird, was delighted to have fresh eggs for breakfast, and would dart upon them with avidity.

CHAPTER XX

CANARY CHARACTERISTICS

Among my canaries were two hybrids, who were half-goldfinch and half-canary. They were fine, dark birds, more like their wild parent than their domesticated one.

While I had my farm I let all my wild birds fly away, except old Bob, the robin. I deliberated about the hybrids, and finally decided to let them take their choice, so after keeping them on the farm for a year I one day opened the door and told one of them that he might fly away with the goldfinches, purple finches, and other birds I had just released.

He went happily, and I heard later that he had called at a farmhouse farther down the road. I hope that he found his wild kindred and migrated with them. I did not know whether to let the other one go or not. He was a fierce little creature, with a beautifully marked goldfinch back, but his spirit was Norwich's—that is, the nervous part of it was. Norwich was never cruel. He had in addition to this mental excitability, inherited Norwich's peculiar leg feathering, and he was the only one of Norwich's descendants that had done this. There was the little, dark fluffy skirt above the clean goldfinch legs, and he also danced while he sang his exquisite and constant song. A bird-dealer once coveted him, for hybrids are valuable, but I decided that nothing would induce me to imprison in a cage this little, wild, free spirit.

One day I found him beating a canary so severely that I said to him, "You are too bad for a house, go and play with your goldfinch brothers." It was the Fourth of July I remember and, opening the door, I pointed to the tall maples about us. He went out with no apparent reluctance, but he would not leave the farm, and for the rest of the day he flew about the house, striking the aviary windows and calling to the birds inside.

When night came he flew to one of the trees. The next morning he resumed his siege of the house, and I had to give in. "Come back," I said, opening the hall door, "if you are as fond of your half-brothers and sisters as that, rejoin them. I will never put you out again."

He came in like a feathered streak, and I have him to-day— nervous, lively, in fine physical condition, and improved in his conduct, as I have never seen him strike a bird since.

This change of temper I have often observed in birds. In the case of this hybrid it was very striking, for, in the days of his youth, he would violently beat an inoffensive bird, and when he grew older I have seen him put up with every insult from another canary who coveted his mate, and who persecuted him from morning till night. Possibly birds, like human beings, gain wisdom with age. He and his mate build nest after nest that I never interfere with, for the eggs of hybrids are said never to hatch.

I have referred to the weak strain in the canary Minnie's constitution and, strange to say, several of her nestlings succumbed before I lost her. I was in a measure prepared for her death, but when I at last found her little dead body I mourned sincerely and a long time, for a stouter-hearted, braver spirit never existed in a fragile body. She always reminded me of a little, plain-featured, delicate woman in a household, who with iron will sways every one to her wishes.

My nervous Norwich sang at the top of his voice on the day that he was made a widower. At the time I thought him heartless. Now I think he was probably mourning in his excitable way. It is as easy to misjudge birds as human beings.

A recent writer says that the Japanese often giggle when a funeral procession passes by. In reality, they are as sympathetic as we are, but they have a different mode of expressing themselves.

After Minnie died, Norwich devoted himself principally to a canary called Pussy's Baby—her mother having been a good-sized yellow bird, with the reputation of a murderess of other canaries. Pussy's Baby never had the influence over Norwich that Minnie had, and he became fussy and meddlesome. He interfered with other birds in their nest-making, and often received rebukes and hard blows. One evening I noticed that he was particularly excited about a new canary that I had put on the roof-veranda. The hybrid led her to his corner, and Norwich followed. The hybrid showed signs of terrible impatience, but as I have stated before, he was a reformed bird, and I did not think he would strike Norwich unless he was cunning enough to wait till I had left them for the night. However, I was shocked to find Norwich's dead body on the floor the next morning, close by the hybrid's perch. He was far from his own nest. Pussy's Baby was sitting on a nestful of eggs in Sukey's room. Norwich should have spent the night near her. He had either fallen dead in one of his fits of frantic singing and dancing, or the hybrid had struck him a fatal blow.

We should not criticize Norwich too harshly. His death was a real grief to the family, and my mother mourned for him as she has mourned for no other bird. He knew her, and when she spoke to him he always put his handsome head on one side, peeped from under his crest, and answered her with an intelligence she could not mistake.

Alas! the dead are soon forgotten (among canaries). Norwich's funeral was held at ten o'clock, and by noon a goldfinch had slipped into his place, and was sitting by Pussy's Baby, devotedly putting choice morsels of food down her pretty, yellow throat.

I was very fond of my goldfinches. They were such neat, dapper, soldierlike little birds, and so good-tempered as they flew about the aviary with their sweet notes. I never saw one of my real goldfinches strike or hurt another bird. This particular one became a good mate to Pussy's Baby, and helped her bring up Norwich's family.

I am exceedingly interested in studying the descendants of Norwich and Minnie, in tracing in the children the characteristics of the parents. It is easy to study canary families, for the young birds hatched this year will next year bring up families of their own, and one has a number of canaries spread out before him.

My Germans have crossed with the English breed, and now I have the mixed families with complications and ramifications. With birds it is as with human families—as the parents are, so will the children be.

Some time ago a lady brought me a little paper parcel.

"This is a dead bird," she said, "but it is so beautiful I want you to look at it."

I did look, and there lay an exquisite little creature with Norwich's heavy crest and lovely, silky feathers, but with Minnie's frail and delicate body.

"You gave it to me when it was a young one," the lady continued, "and the other day I found it dead. I wonder what was the matter with it?"

I had lost sight of the bird, and did not know what care she had given it, but my conclusion was that the weak maternal strain had been the cause of its sudden death.

However, good stock will not survive everything. The most astonishing ignorance prevails with regard to the care of birds. I have had a woman ask me seriously whether it was wrong to change a bird's drinking-water every day.

I wanted to say, "Woman, where is your common sense?" However, I restrained myself, and she went on to say, "A friend of mine had a little bird in a cage and she changed its drinking-water every day and it died, and another friend who had a bird changed the water only once in three days and the bird lived."

Here was a perplexing case.

However, I laid down some broad and generous rules: "Give a bird fresh food and water every day. If he is caged, don't let him stuff himself, but(197) if the cage is a good size, as it should be, he can stand quite an amount of food and green stuff, and a daily bath.

"Better than keeping birds in a cage, is to have one end of a room wired off for them. They are far happier and are less likely to have vermin, and they can eat more. My birds eat an immense amount of green food, and I have never had a case of typhoid fever among them. They have fruit all the year round, and in winter I plant bird-seed for them and give them the green sprouts. They are very fond of the common buckwheat, sown thickly in pots and set in the aviary. They eat down the green shoots in a short time, then I overturn the pots and let them have the mud with the worms and roots in it to play with. This is a great opportunity for my old Bob to get nesting material.

"Always buy the best of seeds for your birds. Don't get seeds in packages. They may be fresh, and again they may be stale. Go to a bird-fancier or a wholesale dealer in seeds. I once gave my birds some sunflower seeds that they would not eat. I thought they had taken a dislike to them, until one day I picked up a few seeds and cracked them. There was nothing inside. I had to open the seeds to find out. The birds knew without opening them.

"Don't hang birds in bright sunshine, except for a short time. Do you like to sit in the burning sun? Treat your birds as you treat your children. Give them light, some liberty, and amuse them. Birds like variety as much as we do. I try to give mine something to interest them.

"Be sure to see that a new bird knows where to find his food. I had an exquisite little goldfinch starve to death in the midst of plenty because I had not penetration enough to discover that he was too stupid to find out where his food dishes were."

I once had a bird come to me suffering from the effect of loneliness. His owner had gone to the country, and the neglected bird had sung all day in a lonely house. He had been used to the sound of children's voices and the care of his mistress. When they left him he was alone except for the space of time required to put fresh seeds and water in his cage. He moped, and was brought to me in a dying condition. So nervous was he from the long hours alone that he started if I went near him. Nothing consoled him, and he soon died.

A canary is a high-strung, nervous, intensely affectionate and faithful bird, and it is pathetic and horrible to reflect how many are tortured to death by the kindest-hearted but most ignorant persons. Bird-dealers give a few directions about the care of birds to persons who buy, but these directions should be in printed form, and should go with the bird.

I can assure purchasers that they suffer loss by not having intelligent instruction. They buy a canary and he dies. They buy another and he dies. I don't suppose many persons get a good singer for less than five dollars. Twenty-five cents will procure a book of instructions. If birds must be kept in cages these books should be consulted, but better than a cage is partial liberty for a canary.

Do you not often see a canary in a cage stretching his wings? What is that for? God gave him his wings for use. If the bird had been intended to hop through life he would have been differently constructed. I never put a bird in a cage so small that he cannot use these wings, and I always allow a caged bird the occasional privilege of flying about the room. At present I have no birds in cages. All are free. In the basement aviary they have fifteen feet by thirty-two of space. From it they enter the elevator that is twenty feet high and ascend to the roof-veranda and sun-room, where are fifteen feet by thirty-two.

Less space than this would do, but I have it, and give it to my birds that now only number forty-five, for I have allowed a number their liberty. Better than cages, better than aviaries is the broad blue sky, and the boundless fields; but of course, one cannot release delicate foreigners in our Northern climate.

CHAPTER XXI

LITTLE PETERS

Soon after starting my aviary I bought a pair of large green parrakeets, and consequently became interested in the whole parrot tribe. I found that there are two hundred varieties or more of the little tropical beauties called parrakeets or little Peters.

This first pair of mine I think, consisted of specimens of the all-green parrakeet or the tirika—a species inhabiting eastern Brazil. In that country these pretty green birds associate in countless flocks, disporting themselves in the forest or swooping down on maize and rice fields.

The lady in Halifax from whom I bought these, said that she found it impossible to keep them in a cage. They would break out and invariably amuse themselves by gnawing the plaster from the walls of the room they were in. At first they did not like me. Parrots, we all know, are narrow in their affections, and rarely like more than one person at a time. They threw me suspicious glances and absolutely refused to be separated from each other. If one flew across the aviary the other uttered a piercing scream, then flew after him.

I took great interest in watching them. They seemed to have quite an amount of individuality, and to be very unlike other birds, both in appearance and in habits. Their hooked beaks, curious claws, awkward gait, their gorgeous plumage, and their queer ways, set them in a class by themselves. They never mingled with birds outside their family. They were my exclusive set.

Parrakeets are not recommended for aviaries on account of their wicked beaks that can so easily break the legs of small birds. This first pair did not trouble me by meddling with other birds, nor did subsequent pairs that I obtained. They always ignored the other inhabitants of the aviary. My parrakeets and doves were all very much wrapped up in themselves, and rarely meddled with their companions, unless they transgressed bird etiquette by pressing close to them.

Most unfortunately, one of these tirikas was found dead a few months after I obtained them. There was a mystery surrounding his death, and I think it must have been the result of an accident. I was so sorry for the lonely survivor, that I took him up to my own room, where he soon became so tame and so lazy that he would not feed himself, but called to me to put favorite morsels in his beak. Rowdy I called this one, and after I had him a little longer I bought a pair of the best known of all the little peters—undulated grass, or shell parrakeets. These Australians were beautiful grass-green and yellow birds, about as large as canaries, but with very long tails. They are often called love-birds, but they are not true love-birds. Genuine love-birds are natives of Africa, and have short tails.

The Australians naturally first came from Australia where immense flocks of them used to be captured while feeding on the seeds of tall grasses. From Australia to Europe was a long journey for them, and after a time bird-keepers found that they could easily raise these pretty creatures in aviaries. In a wild state they make nests in the holes of old trees, or in almost any cavity. In aviaries, if the husk of a cocoanut is given to them, or a hollow bit of wood, they will lay from four to seven white eggs, and soon hatch young ones.

They are lovable and affectionate, and while the female is on the nest her mate sits on a twig near-by and sings his best song, or rather he warbles to her, for they do not sing as other birds do, but make a chuckling, amusing little noise that sounds like talking.

I heard of this devotion of shell parrakeets, but my pair did not act in this way. They kept together a part of the time, but I felt convinced that if separated they would not die of grief. I soon made up my mind that they were two male birds, and this decision was confirmed by their actions when I one day had brought to me a pair of Madagascar love-birds. Now I saw my Australians in their true character. Their names were Big Eyes and Little Eyes, and as soon as Little Eyes saw Mrs. Madagascar he flew excitedly to meet her, followed her from tree to tree, and warbled and gabbled until he brought on a most ludicrous situation of affairs.

All summer we were treated to exhibitions of infatuation, impatience, jealousy, and resentment. Little Eyes was, of course, the infatuated one, Mrs. Madagascar was impatience personified, her mate was jealousy, and the neglected Big Eyes was resentment itself.

The little green Madagascars would sit pressed close to each other, parrakeet fashion, and Little Eyes taking care to get always, on the right side would slip up close to Mrs. Madagascar and warble soft invitations in her ear to leave her mate and come and play with him.

At first she would pretend not to hear, then she would get impatient and would gurgle an impatient aside to her mate, "What a rude bird—what does he want?"

At this Mr. Madagascar would wake up, lean over, and give Little Eyes a dab.

He did not care; sliding off for a minute he always returned. I often pointed out the comical sight to visitors to my aviary— the two Madagascars sitting, trying to sleep away the lovely warm days, Little Eyes in close attendance, whispering and warbling in the tiny green ear next him, and Big Eyes always in the background, grumbling angrily to himself that no one wanted him.

After I had had the Madagascars for some time they

became troubled with overgrown beaks, and one morning I caught them and trimmed the beaks with a penknife. The Australians were nearly frantic to see that I had deprived them of their playmates, and flew about the veranda, chattering and screaming excitedly.

When I showed them the cage containing the Madagascars, they flew right up to it, and Little Eyes, whose love for Mrs. Madagascar had been made fonder by absence, shrieked something that sounded like, "Where have you been? speak! speak!"

The Madagascars, who had been apathetic and frightened while having their beaks trimmed, roused themselves at this warm greeting from their playmate, and one of them squeezed through the bars of the cage. I let the other out, and then there was a jubilation—calls and screams of delight, and a wild dashing to and fro.

Poor Mr. Madagascar soon died. The autumn came, and I think I let them stay out too late, and I also think that the overgrown beak had been left too long. He had not been able to crack a sufficient supply of seeds. I had always a hard time to get my birds indoors in the autumn. They wanted to stay outside, and I have seen a canary sitting on eggs with snowflakes flying around her.

Now that the male Madagascar was gone, Little Eyes' opportunity had come; he kept close to the bewildered widow, warbling, "I am here, I am here—speak quick, speak quick!"

She did speak quick, and the little fellow never deserted her, and was inconsolable when she left him.

Her departure was taken in a most peculiar and tragic way. I had her with Little Eyes and Big Eyes on my farm. I noticed one day that Mrs. Madagascar was gnawing a hole in the plaster, and some one in the family suggested that possibly it would be as well not to allow her to destroy the wall.

"She wants to make a nest," I said. "She will only pierce

a small hole."

I knew she did not need the plaster, for I was always careful to have lime, crushed shells, grit, and sea-sand for my birds.

After a good-sized hole had been made, Mrs. Madagascar only appeared at intervals. I was most pleased at the thought of raising young parrakeets, but one day when confined to my room, I was made slightly uneasy by hearing a scratching in the wall of the bird-room under me.

A few days later I made an investigation, and Mrs. Madagascar was missing—I never saw her again. A Japanese robin was also missing. He was a nervous, fussy fellow, not allowed to associate with the other robins from his country. He had probably seen the hole in the wall, had gone in and investigated, and had lost his way and perished. His would be the noise I heard. Mrs. Madagascar was a quiet bird. She must have died some time before; she had probably lost her way while fussing about her nest, taken a wrong turn, and had gotten bewildered in the partition.

I felt terribly. There was no sound in the wall now, and it was too late to do anything but reluctantly to fasten up the hole so that no other bird could get in. If we had torn down the plaster we might not have found the little bird bodies, for in their bewilderment they might have groped blindly far from the small entrance. If I had only had some of the family make an examination of the wall when I first heard the noise—if I had only been a little more uneasy. It seemed a horrible way for my pretty birds to die. At last I stopped worrying. It would do no good. The birds were gone. But I must be more careful in the future. Little Eyes did not live long after the disappearance of the bird he loved so well, and Big Eyes soon followed him to the bird world, where I hope little birds and big birds have none of the worries and sufferings they experience here.

I was more fortunate with my next parrakeets that are well

and happy at this present time. The first one arrived one cold November afternoon. A lad brought him to me in a box, and said a young man in the north end of the city had sent it to me. Would I please cure it? It was very sick. I opened a box and found a brilliant green African love-bird with a bright red face. Its body was cold, its head and neck were flabby, its claws were curled tightly, its heart was beating very feebly, and it was evidently dying.

I seated myself by the fire, and called for my sister, who was almost as much interested in my birds as I was. In a trice she had a cup of hot water at my elbow, and I dropped a little in the bird's beak. Then she got a hot water bag and I laid the bird on it, face downward, keeping its back to the fire, then I uncurled the little claws that were clenched, for they kept the body from the contact of the bag. At this, the bird showed his first signs of animation, and opening his eyes he feebly tried to bite me. Very much pleased at this sign of life I gave him some warm sweet oil, and after a time a few drops of milk.

His heart action had improved, and soon he straightened himself out and perched on my finger. I then took him up to Sukey's room, thinking that the voices of the few birds I had there might rouse him. They did, and leaving my hand he climbed on a tree, but instead of seeking food he put his head under his wing. I knew this would not do, so I brought him down by the fire again, and offered him a dish of seeds—flax, domestic and French millet, canary, and hemp.

He tried to eat but he was too weak. The seeds fell out of his beak. I offered him apple, and he tried to scrape off some of that, but could not. I masticated some, and he began weakly to nibble at it. When he finished, I again put the seeds before him. He chose the millet; I suppose he liked the soft shell and oily taste. He ate slowly but steadily, but he was still so weak that he would only open his eyes to pick up a seed, and would close them as he ate it.

I still sat by the fire, as he liked the heat, and held him on my finger. To my delight he so far improved that he at last seized a good-sized piece of apple and ate it. I put him in a cage at last, as I got quite stiff from sitting so long in one position, and the love-bird was far enough on the road to recovery to be able to climb unsteadily to a perch, where he sat meditatively, and at last opened his eyes and began to make his toilet for the night.

A bird that is too weak to clean his beak is a pretty sick bird. Red-face now began to pay a little attention to his dirty one, and stroked it gently against the bars of the cage to clean it. Then he began to play with his feathers and cunning little claws.

"He will live," I said triumphantly, and I watched him as he ate at intervals till ten o'clock in the evening. Then I put his cage on the hot water pipes in my study. I had some canaries in there, and seeing them, he spread his wings and started warbling. He looked such an exquisite little creature that, as soon as he was tucked away for the night, I went to my natural history to find out something more about him. This red-headed love-bird seems to be the best known of the parrakeet tribe after the Australian or grass parrakeets, such as Big Eyes and Little Eyes. I learned that they, when excited, spread out their short green tails, tipped by spots of orange and black. Subsequently I saw my own birds doing this—opening and shutting their short tails just like brilliant fans.

They are only six inches long and inhabit forests in the central parts of Africa. There they fly in large flocks, and often sit closely together in long rows, where their gorgeous little green bodies and red faces must produce a very striking appearance. They are said to be the most hardy of the parrakeet family and will stand a good degree of cold weather. They are no bathers, but they take great pride in arranging their feathers, and in pluming and in stroking one another.

Later on, I noticed that this parrakeet did occasionally step into the water and make a pretense of bathing, but what he liked better was to stand near some bird that was taking a vigorous bath and catch the drops as they flew out of the basin. In such cases he would get quite excited and would dip backward and forward as if he too were really in the water.

I was very much afraid that my little Red-face would die, and the next morning hurried downstairs so early that I had to strike a match to see whether he was dead or alive. When he heard me he took his rosy head from under his wing and fell to eating. He got on so well during the day that toward night I took him up to Sukey's room so that he might have the little birds there to cheer him up.

At the sight of these little birds and Sukey he became so excited that I had to bring him back to the few canaries and the quiet of my study. A sick bird is like a sick person—quiet and warmth are necessary for a perfect recovery.

As the days went by he kept on improving, and I learned his history. Some of the Canadian soldiers who went to South Africa to take part in the war against the Boers had brought back this little captive, and had given him to the young man who sent him to me. Who owned him in Africa or how old he was, I could not find out. His owner said that he was inclined to be a delicate bird, and as he had not time to fuss with him I might keep him if I wished. I was most pleased to have him, and found him a great ornament in my aviary. Contrary to the popular opinion that one love-bird will not live alone, Red-face kept in the best of health and spirits, and as there were now no other parrakeets in my aviary, he chose a red-headed Brazil cardinal for a friend. The cardinal hated him, and beat him if he went too near, so Red-face calmly gave him up and spent his days flying about the aviary and warbling happily to himself.

I was so sorry for what I considered his state of loneliness that one day, seeing a rosy-faced love-bird in town, I bought him and brought him home. In order that the two might become acquainted I put them in a cage. They got on pretty well together, but when I took them out Red-face beat the stranger.

In order to illustrate the vagaries of birds, I may say that the Brazil cardinal that hated Red-face and drove him away, allowed the stranger that looked exactly like him to sit near his nest. There is nothing but human nature that at all resembles the doubled and twisted workings of bird nature.

Red-face and the stranger were separated this autumn. When I left home I thought that my pretty Africans would be better off in a large American aviary under the care of a skilled curator, so I attempted to catch them both. The stranger hid and is still at home. I only got Red-face. He is in New York State, and his fate is unsettled, for in the aviary to which I sent him, the gray-headed love-birds object so to his presence that it was feared he would be killed. So he is still seeking a home, and it is possible that he may once more find himself back in Canada with his former bird companions.

CHAPTER XXII

CRESTED CARDINALS

I shall never forget the day that I bought my first cardinals.

I stood in a Boston bird-dealer's shop, looking about me at the great variety of birds. I knew but few of them by name, but I loved them all and wanted them all.

I was most anxious to have a talking minor—the glossy, dark bird that is the only one that will reply when spoken to.

On learning that he was twenty dollars, I said that I could not afford to get him.

A showy redbird that looked too big for his cage next impressed me. He had a black forehead and chin, a jaunty crest, and a vigorous air, and his every movement proclaimed the cruelty of imprisoning so active a bird

"What is his name?" I asked.

"Virginia Nightingale."

James Lane Allen's charming story about this red cardinal came to my mind, and I said I would take him. I think I paid four dollars and a half for him.

An equally attractive bird was one that sat more quietly in his cage—a beautiful gray bird with a red crest and a red bib. I found that he was a cardinal from Brazil, and I said I would take him to be a companion for the other. Alas! I am no seer, and did not anticipate that my two princely birds with their red heads would become mortal enemies.

In addition to the Brazil, whose price was about the same as that of the all-red cardinal, I bought a pair of Java sparrows. They were so neat and handsome with their little gray bodies and their conical beaks, and white ear-tufts, making them look like tiny old men with big pink noses, that I could not resist them.

However, I did not like their ruffled plumage and the bare places on their heads. All Java sparrows, when in condition, should be as smooth as marble.

The dealer assured me that they had only been pecking each other. I believed him then. I would not now. I never saw Java sparrows pull out each other's feathers, and a bare head to me at this time means disease or vermin.

However, I got the little birds and was pleased to learn something about them. They seem to be a kind of English sparrow in their native country, and do an immense amount of damage to the rice crops, eluding the natives who try to capture them. They have a very happy, "chuckie, chuckie," note, as they fly about an aviary. I have never heard them warble, but they are said to do so.

To return to the cardinals. I took them with the Javas in the train with me to Canada, and suffered many pricks of conscience in so doing. I know how hateful and terrifying railway travel is to birds. Had I done right to subject them to it? Well, if I had not bought them in order to give them freedom in a large place, some one would probably have got them and forced them to spend the rest of their lives in tiny cages.

The cardinals were apparently none the worse for their day and a half in the train. When I opened their traveling-cages, they sprang out, ran over the earth in the aviary, then spread their handsome wings and flew to tree branches.

I think they were a little surprised at finding they had room enough to spread their wings. I did not know how long they had been caged. One of my most exquisite pleasures is to release a bird captive, either in my aviary or in the open, then to watch him and imagine what his feelings are.

I probably project a little too much of my own personality into bird bodies, but by dint of drinking and eating, sleeping, playing, and passing day after day with bird companions, I feel myself enabled to interpret some of their bodily and facial expressions, and I can surely and safely say that the uncaged bird is a happy bird. My Javas did not stand the journey so well as the cardinals. One of them was weak and ill, and instead of putting it in a warm, quiet place with its food and water close at hand, I dosed it with a few drops of brandy and water and killed it.

This was a blow to me, and out of that failure and many others arose an intense sympathy for the medical profession. Later on, I naturally became more experienced in treating sick birds, but often the question arose: Here are two remedies. One may mean life, the other death. Which shall I adopt?

At present I practise the Chinese method—I doctor the patient before he gets ill. In China physicians are said to be paid to keep their patients in health, and when sickness comes fees are withheld.

All my energies are bent toward keeping my birds in good health, and at intervals they are caught and examined. I practise with birds the same method that I advocate in the treatment of children—save the child before he is lost. That is the only way to have healthy stock of any kind.

Adults who are hard-hearted never bring me a bird. Little, tender-souled children constantly bring bird patients to my hospital. "These children must rob nests," a skeptical neighbor once remarked, as she observed children coming toward my house with birds.

"They do not," I said decidedly. "I assure you that children often bring me birds at great inconvenience to themselves. They are on their way to the park or the harbor. They discover a robin or a sparrow, a finch or a yellowbird fallen from a tree. They turn back and bring it to me. One little lad going to school the other day, found a sparrow and came to me with it. He was in a great hurry, but he thought it his duty to look after the bird.

"If children are trained to be kind to birds when they are young, they will make laws for their protection when they are grown up, and will save the committal of a vast amount of cruelty and also enormous financial loss to the country by the destruction of insect-eating birds."

I hope I convinced my neighbor. If she was open to argument, I did. If she was closed to it, I did not. Some dear, good people adopt the Scotchman's knock-down policy: "When you see a boy, give him a crack. If he hasn't just been committing some mischief, he is about to do it."

All my boy neighbors were kind to my birds, and last year they did a very thoughtful thing for them.

They knew that I was in the habit of renewing the trees in my aviary every few months by burning old ones and getting some of the colored people about Halifax to bring in fresh ones from the country.

Last New Year's the boys asked me if I did not want their Christmas trees. I said I would be delighted to have them, and one Saturday morning the boys and girls had a regular jubilee running round the snow-covered streets dragging the discarded trees after them, and shouting to other boys to call at the neighbors' and see if they had not some to give away.

Some trees were put in the basement, others were dragged gaily through the halls and up the staircase through Sukey's room to the roof-veranda. The birds sat in corners whispering and talking softly, for they knew the boys quite well and understood that the changing of the trees meant great amusement and occupation for them.

After the children left I walked about the aviary and glanced gratefully at the sweet-smelling evergreens. The birds were busy with exploring expeditions, for each tree had sticking to it bits of tinsel, twine, or wax. What a story each one might tell if it could speak, of happy children dancing round its gift-laden branches.

When I brought home my showy cardinal birds all my boy neighbors liked them. They were both fine singers, though the bird-books give the most of the praise to the Virginian. He had a powerful, and not always sweet song, and sometimes it came in ong bursts, when it seemed as if the violence of his execution would rend his lovely red body apart.

He always wound up with a "Chew, chew, chew!" rendered as vigorously as if he had teeth. I knew he was lonely, for he absolutely and contemptuously refused to associate with his far-away cousin, the Brazilian, and there was no other bird suitable for him in the aviary. So I sent to Boston for a mate for him, and also for one for the Brazilian. I called the Virginian, Ruby, and the Brazilian, Red-top. I regretted the latter name. I should have chosen one to better express the smart, elegant appearance, the pretty manners, and shy, aristocratic ways of this attractive foreigner.

I loved Ruby, but I adored Red-top, and I liked his song better. There was not so much of it, and it was not so loud, but he sang nearly all the time. I called him a conversational singer, for as he walked or ran over the earth—he rarely hopped—he kept his pretty head moving from side to side, and talked or sang constantly to himself. "Dee, dee, dee!" he would say, as he picked up a piece of sand. "Dee, dee, dee!" he would go on, as his runs brought him within reach of an orange or a grape, then he would stop an instant to extract some juice with his strong conical beak.

He had a pair of very smooth dark legs and claws, and always reminded me of a famous French singer who wears long black gloves with her evening gowns. Red-top's elegance was really Parisian, and we all know Brazilians are fond of Paris; then he had a quick, sharp way of saying something that sounded like the French "voyons!"

I never became tired of watching this pretty bird, and would praise him unstintedly to his face, for it never seemed to spoil him. The bold Ruby, on the contrary, if too much petted, would attack some smaller bird, and "show off" as spoiled children do.

I studied Red-top and found out his tastes. He was a great dandy, and extravagantly fond of a mirror. I put a hand-glass in the aviary, and he spent half of his time in front of it, talking, singing, bowing, tapping it with his beak, and running to and fro before it on his trim dark legs. He thought there was a bird in the glass, for he often paused in his song and listened as if to say, "Why don't you respond, bird in the glass?"

One day he made a nest before it and slept in it every night with his beak touching the glass. I tried moving the glass and nest from place to place, and he would follow them wherever they went. Thinking to please him, I put a rose-colored lining in the nest. It was not so bright as his crest, but it drove him far away, and I had to take it out.

"How pleased he will be to see another Brazilian," I said to myself, and in a few weeks I had the felicity of opening another traveling-cage and allowing another Brazilian to step out and confront my elegant Red-top. At first they looked exactly alike to me, except that the new bird's plumage was rumpled in appearance, causing me to name her Touzle.

I soon found that Touzle was gentle and timid in disposition, her eyes were smaller, or rather she kept her eyelids closer together than Red-top did, and that altogether she was one of the best and sweetest birds in my aviary—and how did Red-top treat her?

Alas! The bird world, like the human world, is full of surprises. Instead of flying to her with joy and greeting her as a beloved friend and companion from the far-off Brazilian country, Red-top began to beat her constantly, rudely, and systematically.

"Why, Red-top; I am ashamed of you," I said in amazement. "What do you mean by beating that beautiful, gentle bird?"

He bowed his red crest, sang impatiently something that sounded like, "I can't help it; I can't help it!" and went back to the glass.

I had an illumination. He had mated with the bird in the glass. I took it from him, and soon he stopped beating Touzle—though for a time I had to separate them—and little by little began making advances to her until at last they became such good friends that they never left each other even for one minute.

If Ruby chased them and drove one to the other end of the aviary there would be anxious calls and whistles, and they would hasten to rejoin each other. I was very much interested in their way of greeting each other, even after a few minutes' separation. They would bow profoundly, expand the tail like a fan, and each one would sing a little song. It was a very pretty bird ceremony. I have seen reunited birds salute each other by a cry of delight, a rub on the head with the bill, a sharp tap of affection, such as some parrakeets give, but I never saw any other of my birds bow and curtsy as the Brazil cardinals do.

The first year I had Touzle they made no nest. The summer before she came, Red-top had made a fine nest in a fir tree, weaving long grasses in and out, and shaping it perfectly. The second year they made one or two nests, but laid no eggs. While on the farm they made several nests, laid eggs, hatched young ones, and every time either Ruby or the mockingbird killed their nestlings.

Two years ago I had them up on the roof-veranda where I could watch them, and they hatched two fine, plump young birds. Most unfortunately I went too near the nest one day and the young ones seeing me sprang out, and though I put them back, they would not stay in the nest. They had long legs and jumped like frogs, and fearing that they would spring out during the early morning and become chilled, I took them in the house.

Of course, after removing them from the parents I had to feed them. Raising young birds, especially insectivorous ones, is a delicate matter, and after a week or two they languished and soon died. The little creatures knew me, and would cry for food, and it seemed to me that I could not give them up. They were so intelligent, so pretty, so like their parents.

Their attachment for me did not spring alone from their knowledge that I fed them. A young mouse taught me a valuable truth with regard to the upbringing of the young of any creature. The mouse was found wandering over the floor of my study, too young and too foolish to escape. My sister picked him up and we gave him food, drink, and shelter, yet he did not prosper.

"He is lonely," I said at last, "he wants petting," and I put him up my sleeve.

Now he was happy. He crouched close to my arm, only sticking his little nose out to get kind words and morsels of food I tucked up after him.

A young bird is like a young animal, I concluded. They all want petting and mothering when taken from their parents. Later on, I tried this plan with the greatest success. After feeding young birds I would talk to them, tuck them in their nests, and I soon saw by their playful ways with me that affectionate attention was as necessary as the feeding.

This last summer the Brazilian cardinals built another nest on the roof-veranda. I had a thick, leafy screen in front of it, and did not go near it. Weeks went by, and one fine June day I heard the well-known Brazilian baby-cry in the nest.

I would scarcely allow my family to look at the tree. The birds did not mind the noise of the children in the near-by gardens, the street cars, and guns, whistles, and military music of our garrison and maritime town, but they did not want us to go near them. Our self-denial was soon rewarded, and one day I had the long-waited-for pleasure of seeing a fully fledged young Brazilian step from his nest.

He was a little beauty, gray and white, and with a golden brown, not scarlet crest. I looked forward with interest to his baby moult and acquisition of the cardinal's red hat. His hoarse cries for food were very amusing, and both parents fed him devotedly for some time after he left the nest. He was inclined to be shy, but after a time came out from the shelter of the trees, advanced toward the tempting food-dishes, explored the bathtubs, and had a good dip, flew all about the roof-veranda, and altogether was a very happy little bird until one unfortunate day when I took it into my head to examine one of his claws. It was twisted, and I thought possibly I might do something to straighten it. I caught him, examined it, found I could do nothing to help him, and then placed him on the veranda.

To my dismay, almost to my horror, he could barely move. He hobbled to a corner. He could neither walk nor fly, and crouching in one spot seemed as if he would die. I soon discovered that though I might possibly have hurt his claw in trying to straighten it, the real injury was in the shock to his nerves. I put food and water within his reach and let him alone. Every night I watched him to see that he got under shelter, and in a few weeks he managed to hitch himself up to the higher branches of the trees.

I had waited for four years for a young Brazilian bird, and this was the result. To add to my distress, Touzle, who had built another nest—she started by building an addition to the old one, but fearing vermin I tore it to pieces and she made another—this gentle, amiable Touzle had just before the baby's sad experience with me, begun to show herself in an altogether different light. From being motherly and amiable she became unmotherly and hateful, until I sometimes wanted to shake her.

When the poor cardinal baby, so sorely in need of consolation would, with a nervous and distrustful eye on me, drag himself toward his lovely-looking mother as she sat on her nest in her shady nook, Touzle would daintily step off.

With a look at Red-top she would bow her head, spread her tail and begin to talk to him. Over and over again, whenever the baby came near them, she did the same thing. She urged Red-top on to beat the young one, and drive him away from the nest.

I never saw her look so handsome and so attractive as when she would exhort her mate, and then with him, approach their nestling and drive him out from the shady corner where the nest was.

I suppose this poor afflicted baby did not suffer as much as I thought he did. I hope he did not. I could not help imagining him in the depths of bird despair because his parents had disowned him and I had forfeited his confidence.

Whatever his feelings were, he did what is a very sensible thing for any afflicted mortal to do—he ate and drank, and fought. It did me good to see him lock beaks with his father and stand up to his mother. Many a thrashing he would have got if he had not squared up to the vicious old parents and looked and acted as ugly as they did. He never attacked them, he only defended himself, when to have turned tail might have meant annihilation.

CHAPTER XXIII

CARDINAL BABIES

Bird-lovers who have long waited for the advent of certain young birds will understand my interest in this little fellow. I called him or her, for I did not know the sex, Natal or Natalie, for he was hatched on the twenty-first of June, the natal day of Halifax.

The last thing at night and the first thing in the morning I looked out to the trees on the veranda to see if he were quite safe and comfortable, and I slept with my window wide open so that I could hear any disturbance in the night.

One very bright moonlight night last summer I heard my handsome robin Dixie give a loud shriek of dismay, and begin to fly nervously about the veranda. I find robins are nervous sleepers. The least thing wakens them, and I lay for a few seconds listening to him calling and flying to and fro. When he began to rouse the other birds I sprang up and went softly to the window. I could see nothing, so I spoke to the birds, and when they quieted down, went back to bed.

Presently he started again, and this time some of the birds, instead of merely flying to and fro, began to throw themselves against the wire netting of the veranda.

A panic in an aviary is a serious thing, especially if there are several hundreds of birds who lose their heads at the same time. In my aviary I always have dark corners where birds can fly and hide. I would never put birds under a transparent roof with no place of retreat.

However, this night panic was different from a fright by day. The birds had been violently awakened from sleep, and had completely lost their heads. They had not sense enough to keep in the protected corners when they got in them.

Something unforeseen and startling had occurred, and again I crept softly to the window. I could see nothing out of the way. Of course my mind went to the cats, but since I had had the board put around the elevator, no cat had ascended it.

Finally, I noticed a dark mass behind one of the trees. It was motionless, and I concluded that it was one of the bunches of seed-grass I tossed among the branches for the birds. However, to make sure, I would examine it. I stole across the veranda, and there outside the netting, perched on the railing, was a large black cat looking me calmly in the eyes.

I told her what I thought of her and her family and she took it gracefully. Then I said "Scat," and told her to go down whatever way she had come up.

She coolly retreated a few paces to a Virginia creeper, and swung herself down, as I suppose she had come up—namely, paw over paw.

"The naughty cat has gone, birdies," I said, and went back to my room.

To prove the nervousness of robins, I will only have to say that in a few seconds Dixie was screaming again. This was pure reminiscence. The cat had gone, there was nothing there; but this time he acted worse than he had yet done, and he frightened one bird into hysterics. I heard this one knocking himself against the wire netting like a catapult.

How could any bird head stand that dreadful thumping? I hurried to the spot, and to my dismay discovered that the bird gone crazy with terror was my baby cardinal.

I descended upon him, clasped him in my hand—though I always prefer to catch a bird in a cloth—and absolutely flew to the veranda-room. In there it was dark, and he could not see to beat himself against the windows.

His breath was coming in fluttering gasps—of course he thought the cat had him. I put him quickly on the floor and ran from the room.

I was afraid he was dying. "If I lose him," I said to myself, "how can I forgive that cat?"

I scarcely dared look from my window in the morning; but there, oh, joyful sight! was my beloved baby bird running to and fro along the windows of the veranda-room, trying to get out.

I speedily opened the door, and he flew to his parents, who were delighted to see him.

Strange to say, though they beat him, they would scream angrily at me if I approached too near the little fellow. They kept up a kind of interest in him, though they chastised him.

All day I watched my bird baby, and it seemed to me that nothing for a long time had made me as happy as his escape from death by fright.

I forgave the cat, but the next day I had to call back this forgiveness. I was standing in the middle of the veranda, when I heard, a sound that always strikes dread to my heart. It was a wretched, asthmatic breathing that I have never known a bird to recover from.

Which one was the victim? My eye ran anxiously around my small bird world. Not Red-top; no, he would be the last one I could give up. Not Touzle, the dear mother bird, not Dixie, best and brightest of robins, not his friend the sparrow, not Blue Boy the indigo bunting, nor the goldfinch Boy, nor Andy and his mate, nor any of the sweet-singing canaries. Not old man Java, nor the rosy-faced love-birds, and not, oh, no! not my last, but almost best-loved bird, the cardinal baby.

I stepped near to him and he flew away. The hard breathing stopped, and it seemed to me for a minute that my heart stopped too. I followed him, and the wretched, rasping sound was now quite close to me. My baby was doomed. I would have to give him up. In some brighter, fairer world I might see that pretty creature mature and perhaps live forever—who knows—for many wise men say that there will be a future life for birds, that an all-wise and all-merciful Father will never utterly destroy any created thing that has in it the spark of life.

There was only one thing to be thankful for. I would have time to get acquainted with the certainty of his death—and as far as I could observe, a bird's sufferings were not extreme when afflicted in this way. The canary Britisher had the same trouble, and he seemed to get a great deal of pleasure out of life. So day by day I watched my pet, and delighted in giving him all the dainties he would eat.

He lingered on until I left home in the autumn, but shortly afterward died. I heard that the dear little bird with the reddish-brown crest had been picked up dead on the floor of the aviary.

Poor baby—I cannot think of him without emotion, but to my joy I have dreamed of seeing him well and happy and trotting about among his former companions.

Some one speaks of birds "making sweet music in one's dreams," and I often have the pleasure of seeing my pets about me during my sleeping moments.

Next summer I hope my Brazil cardinals will be more successful in the raising of young ones. I notice that year after year they get tamer and more reasonable.

One morning last August I heard Red-top making a great noise about daybreak. His usual habit during summer is to wake at the first streak of day and begin singing in a whisper, and gradually to ascend into a hearty song. This particular morning he was so noisy that I went to the glass door and said, "You are making a great racket, my boy. Think of the neighbors."

Before I spoke to him he had been swelling out his throat, singing with all his might, "Cheery, deary, wearie, dearie," supposedly, to enliven Touzle on her woven nest near him.

After I spoke to him, he put his crested head on one side, as if to think over what I had said and remarked, "Hi, hi; that's true!" then went off to play with his mirror, singing in a lower key, and tapping it briskly with his beak.

My birds all follow his example of singing before it is really light, then, getting their breakfast later on, when they can see well.

Red-top amused my married sister one day by falling into a trap we set for him. I wanted to catch him for some reason or other, and put some of his favorite dishes into a large cage and tied a string to the door.

He watched me cunningly, and would not go in.

"Please take the string," I said to my sister; "I believe he will go in for you."

I left him, and she said after I had gone he threw her a careless glance, as if to say, "You don't count, you never catch us," and immediately walked into the cage, whereupon she laughed at him and pulled the string.

All my cardinals have been very strong birds, and never for one instant lose their spirit. Whenever I catch one—Virginian or Brazilian—they fight me, bite my fingers, and fall into a rage of resentment without terror. They know I won't hurt them, but they want me to know that they are birds of too high lineage to be handled.

One day Red-top got one leg so tangled in a long bit of twine he was weaving into his nest that he could not move. I had to call my sister to help me cut him free, and he fought us all the time we were engaged in our amiable task.

Another day he got whitewash in his eyes. That too made him angry, and I telephoned to our physician, who told me to wash his eyes with warm water, then put in sweet-oil with a medicine-dropper. The next day I bathed them with boracic acid, and in a short time he was quite well.

So great a favorite with me is this charming bird that for his sake I fall into a state of such sadness when I see his fellows in shop windows that I can scarcely describe my feelings, lest I be taxed with exaggeration. The suffering I experience is perhaps akin to that of the devoted friend or relative of a bright and beloved child who sees another child resembling him in a wretched and unhappy home.

For the sake of the first dear child you shudder as you witness the sad case of the second. So with the Brazil cardinals. I most earnestly hope that the time will soon come when the iniquitous traffic in foreign birds will be stopped. We are protecting our native birds. Why not extend our protection to the helpless, lovely, and interesting foreigners? They too suffer, and beat their young lives away against cruel prison-bars.

Here in this large and kind-hearted city of Boston I saw the other day European goldfinches and linnets going up and down their cages, trying the wires with their little beaks, pleading vainly for freedom. My heart ached as I looked at them.

I often say to bird-dealers, "How thankful I am that you can no longer sell native birds." These men do not care. There are plenty of other birds on the market. Now, if we can only free the unfortunate foreigners, bird-dealers who really love birds will find occupation in bird reservations and large aviaries, for I have come to the conclusion that undomesticated birds should be confined only for some wise purpose, or for scientific research.

I have already said that I ordered a mate for my red Virginian Ruby as well as for Red-top. When she arrived I found that instead of being a rosy-red bird like the male, she was of a dull brownish-vermilion. However, she was a handsome bird, and in fine condition. She darted from her traveling-cage, and the brilliant Ruby fell into the most ludicrous state of amusement, ecstasy, and bewilderment. He acted like a simpleton, flying to and fro after her, twisting his body from side to side, spreading his tail and wings, elevating and lowering his fine crest, singing at the top of his voice, then winding up with something earnestly delivered that sounded like, "What a dear! what a dear!"

All this was going on at the same time that the naughty Red-top was beating poor Touzle. I watched both pairs of birds, and Ruby's bodily contortions were so fantastic that I was overcome with laughter.

He paid no attention to me. He was altogether taken up with the vivacious and handsome Virginia, who would not allow him to come near her. She flew from one end of the aviary to the other, switching her tail from side to side, avoiding him systematically, and making him sleep away off from her when night came.

This shyness did not last. Soon the two were very great friends, and flew about together all day long. Ruby's delight in the companionship of one of his own kind took the form of feeding her. He kept the choicest morsels he found and put in her beak, almost exercising self-denial, for at the time of her arrival I did not have a sufficient supply of his favorite insect food in the aviary. If there was only one worm, Virginia got it.

I don't know whether she appreciated his devotion or not. She was a restless creature, very unlike Touzle, who was quiet and reposeful. Virginia never kept still for any length of time, unless it was the nesting season. Then she sat quietly on her nest, day after day, and week after week.

I had some curious experiences with her, and every season it was the same thing. She made a nest, laid eggs, sat patiently on them till they hatched out, then began to feed the young ones until the day that I found them either on the ground, or laid out in a row on a window-ledge.

I got to dread the sound of young Virginians chirping in

the nest. They were rarely allowed to live more than a few days, and it was painful to find the plump, dead bodies, well-shaped and looking well-nourished. What killed them? I shut up one suspect after another. The gallinules, the mockingbird and Ruby himself. Red-top would not dare to go near his enemy's nest. Not until two years ago did I discover that Virginia herself lifted them out.

This was a blow to the mother-love theory, but I gave her the credit of thinking that the young ones died in the nest, and not being able to endure the sight, she took them out. They were rarely mutilated. They had been carefully carried in her powerful beak.

One day I was shocked to find three young ones about ten days or a fortnight old squirming on the window-ledge. This was downright murder. I revived one, kept him for part of the day, then he died. These were fine young birds with feathers starting.

I puzzled more and more. There was plenty of food in the aviary, and Virginia herself was in fine condition, for she would make three or four, or even five nests a year. This last summer she murdered four sets of young ones. I took a fifth lot from her, but they died on my hands. I had one theory after another to account for this slaughter but none of them was satisfactory. Feeling that another bird-lover might be more successful with her in the nesting season, I sent her this autumn, with Ruby, to a skilled curator of birds, and next summer I shall await results with interest.

I shall miss her and Ruby immensely for, strange to say, the Virginian female possesses a song almost equal to that of the male bird. When she was upstairs and Ruby down below, and they sang to each other, I often sat in my study listening to them and thinking of Mary McGowan's lines with regard to the red cardinal:

No slumber songster he, with vesper warblings low,

But bold his every note, and full and strong:
In his clear ringing pledge, hear him unstop the flow,
Then gurgle forth the red wine of his song.

Virginia never became very tame, but Ruby reminded me of a dog, in his ways. One night I shut him in the furnace-room for some reason or other, but he fretted to get back to Virginia, and after dark I went downstairs with my small candle lantern, for I had to be careful what sort of a light I carried among the dry spruces and firs of the aviary. Ruby was pressed against the wire door. He spoke to me, and I held the lantern close to him and guided his feet back to Virginia. Too impatient to wait he hopped on ahead, and I followed quickly, trying to keep the swinging light steady.

He was so reasonable, so sure of me, so grateful for what I was doing, that I could scarcely refrain from seizing his pretty red body in my hands and caressing him as I do my pet pigeons whom I often wake from their sleep.

When he got near Virginia he climbed into a tree with a satisfied "Tsip!" and I left him.

He was an exquisite night singer; indeed, one of his names is the American nightingale, and one summer I had to request him to descend to the basement to sleep, as his loud night-singing disturbed a delicate neighbor. He was a very mischievous bird, and one day when I was carrying a hammer and nails about the aviary, he espied a match in the box, and darting down, flew off with it for his nest. I pursued him for a long time before I could persuade him to drop the dangerous plaything.

It is a great delight to me to reflect that these lovely cardinals can no longer be bought in the birdstores. How any one can enjoy the sight of this bright red bird, with his wild, free spirit hopping to and fro in the narrow confines of a cage, is as much of a mystery to me as the wearing of his dull and lifeless skin in a hat. We must educate our children into the conviction that a dead bird is as grotesque an ornament as a dead mouse or a dead frog.

CHAPTER XXIV

SPARROWS AND SWALLOWS

Poor little brown immigrants, how many enemies and how few friends they have, and yet what have they done to deserve so hard a fate? Merely following out the biblical instruction to multiply and increase—they always remind me of true Anglo-Saxon stock. They protect the family, they fight all strangers and, "Colonize, colonize," is their motto.

I have had quite an extensive acquaintance with the English sparrow, both in town and in the country, and I think that this bad boy of the air has a worse name than he deserves. Undoubtedly he is bad; so are all boys, and all birds, and all men and women. We want supervision, correction, restriction—but the sparrow has good points.

Sparrow mothers lead all birds in mothering, as far as my observation goes. Again and again I have put a baby sparrow on the roof. He is a stranger picked up in the street. I do not know what nest he comes from, he does not know, no one knows. He is like the poor dog in the express car on a certain railway that ate up his tag. No one knew what place he was bound for.

Well, the instant the lost sparrow opens his little beak and gives a cry of distress, three or four mother sparrows come flying toward him with their beaks full of food. They don't wait to see whose baby he is, as some human mothers would wait. He is a baby, and he is hungry, and they are going to feed him, and they do it until he flutters from the roof, and I have to pick him up and take care of him myself. If I put him in a cage and set him back on the roof, the street sparrows will try all day long to feed him through the bars. Yes, indeed, a mother sparrow is the best mother bird I know.

I have never tried them with the young of other birds, but I have tried their young with canaries. My canaries are the dearest and best of parents to their own nestlings, but none of them will feed the babies of other canaries. As for young robins, yellow warblers, finches, and sparrows, they utterly ignore them, unless they have particularly piercing voices. In these cases the canaries grow nervous and stuff their own young ones as if they thought the cries of distress issued from their throats.

Once I saw a canary hitch up to a young sparrow and look down its throat. He then shook his crest and hopped away, as if to say, "I could never fill that cavity." Two summers ago I put a demure, well-behaved young sparrow baby into a cage of German canaries. She hopped into the nest, settled her little gray body down among the four yellow birds, and unheeding the mother's impatient pushes and shrugs, sat there till she grew old enough to take to a perch. After a time I took her out of the cage and put her on the veranda. She played there all day, but every night she came in to sleep near the canaries.

I knew she was in the room, for she flew out every morning when I opened the screen-door, but where was her sleeping-place? I looked high and low, but could not find her for a long time, until late one night, when I was saying, "I wonder where that bird is?" I saw something move slightly on the top of the canaries' cage. A sheet was thrown over it, and under the sheet was the smallest and flattest projection. I laughed as I looked at it, and said, "I have found it at last."

Every night this quaint little sparrow, Judy by name, had crawled up under the sheet and had slept on the wires of the cage, over her foster-mother and the young canaries. It was a very uncomfortable sleeping-place, and after I found her out she never used it again, but took to a box on the wall near a mirror. There she sat calmly gazing at me night after night as I held up the light to look at her.

She was so interesting that I could not let her go. She seems to recognize a certain kinship with the street sparrows, for she chirps excitedly to them, but she does not care to go out with them, and has chosen for a mate a widowed Java sparrow, who is not so devoted to her as she is to him. He is good to her, however, and flies about with her, but she does all the nest-making. This summer she had a curious structure of straw among some fir branches that she kept adding to, until it was over a foot long. For some months she laid eggs in the middle of this nest. Occasionally I took out a few and gave them to the other birds to eat, but when I lifted the nest down this autumn there were still a dozen in it.

I was sorry she had been too flighty to rear some Java and English sparrow-hybrids. They would have been most interesting. Perhaps she will have more steadiness next summer. I used to be amused with her at breakfast-time. She would lean far out of her nest to see what I was giving to the other birds, then with a joyful sound to her mate that sounded like, "O Java," she would fly down to investigate.

One sparrow I had, learned to sing some of the notes of the Brazil cardinal. The cardinal hated him and beat him frequently, but the sparrow followed him from place to place, and practised his little tune till it was becoming quite perfect. A sparrow is said to have a good vocal apparatus, and I suppose there is no reason why he should not sing if he wants to. Unfortunately, I put this bird out of the aviary, and I have never heard him sing again. Perhaps the birds in the street shamed him out of it.

My sparrows have mostly been good sparrows, and as a class have not been greater fighters than other birds. I have observed them in the aviary and out of it, and have rarely seen them chase or annoy smaller birds. In the city, goldfinches, robins, some warblers, purple finches, and song-sparrows came about the roof-veranda, and talked to the birds inside the netting, and sometimes my canaries go out and fly about, but the sparrows never interfere with them.

On my farm the sparrows were equally good. They never injured the tiny wild birds that came for food, but fed peaceably with them. On neighboring farms sparrows were known to tear swallows' nests to pieces, but they never molested my swallows, though they built close to our house doors. I think possibly the reason lay in the abundance of food scattered about. The little rogues knew that there was enough for them summer and winter. They understood that I liked them, and they did not harm my other pets.

They are most intelligent birds. Living by their wits has developed them amazingly. In Paris I used to be interested with their discrimination in the matter of making friends. An elderly man who fed a flock in the Tuileries Gardens had gained the confidence of every member of it. They would not come to strangers, but when he called "Jeanne! Pierre!" and the rest of their names, each bird would fly to him in turn.

I had a great affection for the skimming swallows about my farm, and often watched them as they caught flies or went to the low ground for mud for their interesting nests. I was very sorry to find that many of these graceful swallows suffered as much from parasites as other wild birds I had known.

One case, on a farm near me, was quite painful for the sufferers. A window in a carriage-house loft had been left open, and a pair of old swallows, finding the rafters a secluded place, built a fine mud nest against them. When the young ones were hatched they were visited every day by the farmer's wife, who grieved to find them attacked by fat worms that mostly crawled into their ears. These worms were half an inch long, had no hair, but possessed rudimentary feet like a caterpillar's, that were only visible under a microscope. One worm penetrated a young bird's nostril so far that only a tiny piece of his body was visible. Enough remained in sight to seize upon, but his forced exit from the nostril was followed by a gush of blood. The sore place soon got well, and the other young swallows also recovered after their ears were cleaned out.

The kind-hearted mistress of the farm destroyed this mud nest, made a new one of excelsior and wool, put the little swallows in it, and the parents, far from being frightened by this radical change in their environment, went on feeding their young ones, conducted them out into the world beyond the carriage house, and came back the next year to nest in the same place.

Two stories about the swallows interested me greatly. The first one was to the effect that the robin was the bird who undertook to teach the first swallow created how to build a nest. I could imagine the fussy, nervous robin entering upon the task with great haste, and it is said that she very quickly got out of patience. Every time she opened her beak to tell the swallow how to choose her mud and sticks, and how to shape the nest, the intelligent bird would say, "I know that; I know that." At last, and unfortunately when the nest was only half finished, the robin became exasperated and flew away, and from that day to this every swallow has to be content with a partial home that often falls to pieces.

The second story was a Swedish one, and relates that when the crucified Christ hung on the cross, a swallow kept flying back and forth crying, "Svala! svala!"—comfort, comfort!

I do not believe in the increase of sparrows, and yet I bring up a certain number of them every year. How can I refuse the children who come to me with the tiny birds and say, "This is our sparrow, please feed him. We will call in a few days to see how he is."

"Children," I often say falteringly, "if this is a sick sparrow, you won't blame me if I chloroform him?"

"Oh, no," they always cheerfully reply, but unfortunately

the sparrow is rarely a sick sparrow. He is usually in the best of health, and he opens his yellow-rimmed beak and stares trustingly at me, and after I give him one meal my fate is sealed. I am nurse-in-chief for many days, though a young sparrow, of all my birds, learns soonest to feed himself. Life is sacred in the eyes of children, and the way to get rid of sparrows is not by inciting boys and girls to destroy them.

The whole department of bird and animal life should be under supervision. We have too many cats and dogs, too many sparrows and pigeons in our cities. The health of the citizens is the first consideration. Each city should maintain bird-houses, and bird reservations. If I can raise shy birds on a city veranda, why could not more wild birds be raised in bird-houses in public gardens and parks?

It would not be an easy matter to thin out the sparrows, or utterly to destroy them, but it could be done, and our wild birds could be enticed back, and less money and time be spent in fighting insect pests. The birds' little beaks will do more effective work than all our spraying and tree-climbing.

It must amuse the birds immensely to see big, clumsy mankind trying to ferret out the gipsy moth, for example. The sparrows do eat some insects' eggs and larvæ, for I have seen them do it inside and outside my aviary—but it is a hopeless task to try to defend these poor little fellows—these "avian rats," these "cosmopolitan pests," as ornithologists call them. I cannot dislike them nor call them names. They are brave little birds, and when I throw open my window on a cold winter morning, and see them waiting on the opposite roofs for their breakfast, and reflect that they alone of all the summer birds are left to us in the city, I cannot deal harshly with them.

Under a certain tree, is emptied each day a certain amount of grain, no more no less, and it is put there whether I am at home or not. Birds like to know what to depend on. They don't want to be fed spasmodically any more than we do. All day the sparrows flutter about the house. As far as I can make out we have a flock of sixty or seventy in our neighborhood. When night comes they tuck themselves away under the house-eaves, getting near the chimneys if they can. When the time comes to exterminate them I will help. In the meantime I do not see what good it would do to carry on an unsystematic and shocking killing of the helpless young ones—the pets of my children friends.

CHAPTER XXV

A MOTHER CAREY'S CHICKEN

Perhaps the strangest pet I had in my aviary was a black bird that was brought to the door one evening by a boy. He said that a young man had picked up this pigeon on the common, and had told him to bring it to me. I found that it was a sooty-looking bird, with a tubular bill and white feathers at the end of its tail—evidently a Mother Carey's chicken—that had probably been flying across the peninsula on which the city of Halifax is built, and had dropped in exhaustion. I saw that it was ill, and as soon as I could, hurried to the fish market and interviewed an old sailor who had fished on the banks of Newfoundland. He told me that flocks of these petrels used to follow his ship, eating the fish livers that were thrown overboard and that floated for days behind them. He had no liver on hand, but he gave me a whiting, for he said that fish would also float on the water.

I knew nothing about these deep-sea matters—I only know Mother Carey's chickens by seeing them follow Atlantic steamers; but finding that the petrel would not eat the whiting, I went back to the sailor and got some liver that he had managed to secure for me.

The petrel would not eat this either, so I called my sister and asked her to kindly get out our feeding-sticks. After cutting up pieces of the liver she took them one by one on her sticks and dropped them into the bird's long bill that I held open for her. After a meal was over I wiped his face and put him on the floor, and he scuttled under the radiator. One day I put him in a bath, but he went right under the water, and I had to take him out.

He never fed himself, and three times a day we got out our sticks and the fish liver. He was gentle but feeble, and was more lively at night than during the day.

When displeased he made a peeping noise, and at all times he possessed a strong and peculiar smell.

I had him for three weeks, and for a time he improved, and would fly low over the floor, ascending and descending as if going over waves of the sea.

I hoped that he would soon get entirely well, so that I might give him his liberty, but he suddenly became very ill and died, regretted on account of his gentle disposition.

We photographed him before losing him, and found him a good bird to pose. Some of our birds were most aggravating when they saw a camera. They were not afraid of it, but they acted like naughty children, getting behind it and under it, and everywhere but in front of it. Many an hysterical laugh have we had when, time after time, just as a successful group of birds, dogs, cats, or hens had been placed in good position, half our pets would get up and saunter away.

At last the sight of the camera produced such a state of merriment in the family that my sister, who had infinite patience with our pets, would send us all away, and manage the four and two-footed creatures alone.

In speaking of unmanageable pets, I must make honorable mention of our fox terrier Billy, who was with the birds so much that he might almost be called an inhabitant of the aviary. He did not love the birds—he was jealous of them—but he never harmed them and, moreover, they knew he would not harm them, and had no fear of him. He never played with them, but he would wallow with Sukey in the accumulation of scraps, seeds, grass, and other rubbish on sweeping days in the aviary, until I have seen the maid gently push them both aside with her broom.

Billy would cheerfully pose when he saw a camera, and follow us whenever we went to the photographers in the town. One day when my mother was having her picture taken, Billy placed himself at her feet. The photographer took him up and lifted him to what he considered a more attractive position.

I shall never forget the look of doggish reproach that Billy gave him as he walked back to his original position, and held it. It seemed to say, "Don't you know, sir, that I am a dog that is used to posing? I know how to show off my good points better than you do."

Strangers sometimes remarked that no member of our family was photographed without this pet dog.

"We cannot help it," we used to reply, "Billy follows us and gets into the picture. We can't keep him out."

Dear little dog! He was the last of the real animals in "Beautiful Joe," to leave us, and a year ago, at the age of sixteen years and a half, lay down one day to die, as calmly and peacefully as he had lived.

CHAPTER XXVI

SWEET-SWEET AND THE SAINT OF THE AVIARY

Among the books that I bought when I started my aviary was one that amused me immensely. It was a clever book, but the description of each bird almost always began with the assertion that this particular bird was the best, the brightest, and the prettiest bird of the entire race of birds.

I have not had the variety of birds described in that book, but now that I am attempting to relate the particulars of some of my pets, I find myself tempted to ascend up to the same heights of eulogy. Each bird is the best bird. Each one is the most beautiful, the most lovable—one has to exercise self-restraint to avoid exaggeration.

I have had quite a large number of birds that I cannot write about at length. I will merely mention some of them.

I one day expressed a wish to have some bluejays in the presence of a bird-fancier, and shortly afterward he arrived with a pair that he had bought from a woman near Halifax, in one of the colored settlements composed of descendants of Southern Negroes. They were handsome birds, and as I released them in the aviary I could not help thinking that if they were foreigners how greatly they would be sought after.

Their appearance in the aviary occasioned the greatest consternation among some of my birds, whose instinct recognized in them hereditary enemies. This instinct of fear in these partly domesticated birds is the same that makes them cower when a hawk passes over their cages.

One indigo bunting fainted and fell motionless on the ground. I took her upstairs where she would not see them, and the other birds soon quieted down, for the blue jays went into a corner and stayed there, only occasionally uttering harsh, unhappy cries.

I wondered how they had ever contented themselves in a small cage with the colored woman, if they were so unhappy in my aviary. I begged them to have patience, that there were fires in the forests about the city, and as soon as they were extinguished I would set my prisoners free.

Finally a bright morning came, when I put them outside the window, and they flew swiftly away, and I hope are living happily in my beautiful native land.

Shortly after they left me, a small boy arrived at our door with a tiny cage, scarcely suitable for a canary.

"I heard you had a pair of bluejays you don't want," he remarked composedly, "and I thought I would take them and keep them in this cage."

I tried to make him view this proposition from the bluejays' point of view, and embraced the occasion of preaching again the doctrine that it is a cruel thing for a boy to rob a bird's nest, or confine a bird in a cage. Also, that I wanted no eggs from nests, and no nestlings, except those that had wandered far from their parents, and who would starve if left to themselves.

I found no trouble in getting boys to understand this. Boys and girls are just what the grown people make them. If we are kind to birds they will imitate us.

Among the small birds that I have owned were some interesting native siskins, that I found languishing downtown in a tiny cage one hot August day. I bought them, and the delight of these wild birds on getting into roomy quarters was very touching.

They flew at once to the spruce and fir trees, and began eating their tips. Subsequently I gave them their liberty, and they raced each other to the tops of the tallest trees they could find.

A smaller bird than the siskin was a tiny, yellow warbler whose eyes seemed unnaturally large for the size of its body. A little girl brought it to me one morning, closely folded in her moist hands.

"It is a weeny thing," she said in an awed voice. "I saw it in our stable. It would not go away, so I walked up to it and put my hands over it, for I was afraid pussy would get it."

"It is one of the many warblers in this neighborhood," I said. "They often come to the wire netting and talk to my birds. I will take good care of it."

I intended to release the little creature as soon as he got rested, but he became so tame and followed me about with such unmistakable devotion shining from his dark eyes that I could not bear to part from him.

Sweet-Sweet I named my new pet, and one Sunday morning I was inexpressibly grieved to find that I had accidentally struck the little fellow as he came too near me.

I picked him up and sprinkled water on him whenever he had a fit or seizure, in which he either lay still or fluttered wildly to and fro. I did not go to church, but devoted myself to poor Sweet-Sweet, and encouraged him to eat when he came out of his spasms. By night-time he was almost well, and next day had quite recovered.

Unfortunately, and to my very great surprise, my bird with the melting eyes was a great fighter, and would attack birds so much larger than himself that I trembled for his safety. He was not nearly so large as my canaries, but he would fight any of them with the greatest intrepidity.

I really should have allowed this little beautiful but mischievous bird to fly away when the autumn came, but I had grown so much attached to him and he was so much at home in the aviary that I could not make up my mind to let him go. I also had a little curiosity to see whether I could keep a warbler all winter.

He got on nicely until one unfortunate day, when he made up his bird mind to bully one of my Japanese robins.

I have never found these robins quarrelsome, but this one deeply resented Sweet-Sweet's interference with the rapid tenor of his way. I was just wondering what I should do with my naughty warbler, for I knew his gay, impatient spirit would fret itself to death in a cage, when one day I found that the Japanese bird had flown into a rage with him, and had almost torn him to pieces.

I was shocked—I can hardly express the short, sharp pain I felt, when I picked up that tiny, beloved bird body. Only a bird, but how dear! If I had only let him fly away with the other yellow warblers to some fair southern land! I selected two of the greenish-yellow feathers, crossed them, and put them in my bird diary with the mournful entry of his death.

Sweet-Sweet had been a worse fighter than any English sparrow I ever saw, and a worse bully and fighter than Sweet-Sweet, was another small bird I possessed for years—a brilliant red, blue, and gold nonpareil.

He was not brilliant when I got him. I had seen pictures of nonpareils, and had asked a bird-dealer to get me a pair. He sent them to me one cold winter evening, and to my dismay, on opening the birds' traveling-cages I found that one of them was diseased, his red neck being bare of feathers.

I wrote the bird-dealer an indignant letter, reproving him for sending a sick bird on a journey, and telling him that I never again would buy a bird from him. The proper way, of course, to discourage the traffic in birds is not to buy them. This dealer probably cared little for my remonstrance.

I put this little sufferer at once into a large cage, with fresh seeds and water. He had a succession of fits, and tumbled and fluttered about his cage. However, in between the fits he would eat and drink, while I sat admiring his courage. When bedtime came he heroically mounted a perch and sat there, so weak that he rocked to and fro for a long time before his little claws got a firm grip of the perch. Finally he was able to put his head under his wing, or back of his wing, as I always wish to say, and went to sleep.

When I read bird stories as a child I always fancied that a bird put the head under the side of the wing next the breast, whereas he reaches back and tucks the head behind the wing. The position looks uncomfortable, but I suppose the bird knows best about that.

As I have said before, I was disappointed in the appearance of these dull, olive-green nonpareils. They were young ones, and I had to wait three years for them to become like the beautiful birds in my books, with the violet heads and necks, the partly red and partly green backs.

They are natives of Mexico and Central America, and rarely get farther north than northern Illinois and Kansas. They used to be trapped in great numbers and shipped to the Northern States, there to languish in captivity. They are partly insectivorous birds, and miss their accustomed diet in cage life. If canaries required insect food they never would have become the highly domesticated birds that they are.

I put my sick nonpareil into the cage with a Java sparrow that was also out of condition. I scarcely thought the new-comer would live through the night, but my mother, who is an early riser, called out to me in the morning that the little Southerner was as "pert" as possible.

I had a hard time with him, as I had also with Java. They both lost all their feathers. The nonpareil was the worst looking bird I ever saw. I called him Baby, and he was soon a naked, skinny, scaly-legged baby, with nothing attractive about him but his soft, dewy eyes. I kept him and Java oiled and secluded in my study. They were not ugly to me, but strangers were apt to burst into peals of laughter at sight of their featherless bodies.

Every night I woke them up about eleven o'clock to take a late supper, for they became rather indifferent about their food, though apparently they did not suffer. I dreaded the long winter nights for them in their enfeebled condition. Java became very tame, and when I tapped the cage and said, "Come out for a walk," he would hop all around the room. Of course, there was no flying for either of them in their condition.

Everything passes with time, and in a few months my birds' purplish-red bodies became dark in hue, then crowds of downy pin-feathers jostled each other. In a short time my hideous little pets were, one, the exquisitely-hued nonpareil, the other the modest gray and white sparrow, with feathers overlapping so smoothly that he looked like a carved bird.

I regret to say his prosperity, instead of sweetening Baby's disposition, soured it, and when I put him into the aviary he speedily took to himself the rôle of persecutor. He was so small that he could not do much harm, but he used to fight continually, often in a very amusing fashion.

One day I saw him attack a fawn-colored, foreign finch that we called the Widow. She was eating seeds from a box, and Baby tried to push her away. The Widow bit him and would not yield. Then Baby seized her tail and pulled it. She did not seem to mind this, so he pulled harder. Then, as she was still indifferent, he fell upon her and gave her a beating and forced her to leave him in possession of the field. This was not serious, but the naughty Baby progressed in wickedness, and finally whipped a timid canary so violently that she died, and also struck a Bengalese finch a blow that was the cause of his death. Bullying was bad enough, but this was murder, so at last I kept the bad little nonpareil in my room the most of the time. He perched on a cage in the wall near my mirror, and seemed to take a certain amount of satisfaction in being with me. He lived for several years, and only died a few months ago. I noticed one day that he seemed very much excited, and

leaving my room flew into other bedrooms—a thing he rarely
did. One morning a little later I found him lying motionless
on the floor. His little mischievous life was over, and I was
sorry for it, for when he was good he was "very, very good."

The saint of the aviary is little Blue Boy, the indigo bunting, alive yet, and prosperous, though I have feared for his life again and again. I never saw him strike a bird. I never saw him do anything naughty. He is quiet and gentle in his habits, never interferes with the other little birds, gets up early, waits patiently for his food till others have finished, retires to quiet corners and sings his little tinkling songs, goes to bed betimes, and if it is a warm moonlight night, is apt to wake up three or four times and sing to himself, not loudly, but loudly enough to cheer any light sleeper.

He never chose a mate. He never seemed to want one. He is the most quiet, self-contained, meek little bird imaginable. If any bird chases him he flies to his little box in my room. The only thing he begs for is a cockroach. He will hop toward me in the morning with a pleading expression, if I have not one of the most unprepossessing members of the beetle tribe for him.

At one time I started cockroach culture in a companion box to that of the meal-worms. My mother was resigned, but doubtful about the experiment, and I noticed that the cockroaches all fell victims to some sudden calamity during one of my absences from home.

However, by diligent search, we can usually find two or three around the hot-water pipes at night, and the maid I have taking care of the birds, writes me that she tries hard to get "a Cockroach every Night for the Little Blue Bird."

CHAPTER XXVII

A HUMMINGBIRD, AND NATIVE AND FOREIGN FINCHES

The bird that paid the briefest visit to my aviary was a hummingbird. I had him for a day, then there was a rush of wings and he was gone. My first experience with this interesting and tiniest member of the bird race was in California. While sauntering one day about the beautiful grounds of the Belmont School a lad said to me, "Come and see a new bird's nest." He took me to a spot close to a rustic bridge where, in the long blades of what we in the East call "ribbon grass," and only a few feet from the ground, a hummingbird had fastened an exquisite, fairylike cup, made of the softest plant down.

There sat the mother bird on two pure white eggs, gazing calmly at the schoolboy who, with a number of his friends, visited her daily. One boy got into serious trouble for, with mistaken zeal, he tried to feed bread-crumbs to the little mother, and brought down on his head a severe reprimand from the older lads.

As I hung over the dainty nest I wondered whether the hummingbird had had an eye for the beautiful, in choosing this spot to bring up her nestlings. Just below her home, a small brook or "creek" as Californians say, ran among great clumps of calla lilies. Among the lilies, lived several frogs, and as we leaned over the rustic bridge above them, we used to call "Little brother," and rouse one fat frog who would respond, "Lit-tle Bro-ther, Lit-tle Bro-ther," till the other frogs would take up the friendly refrain and send it resounding away up the creek.

These schoolboys were the best boys that I ever saw to birds. Two hundred of them went daily to and fro in the finely wooded school-grounds, thirty-five acres in extent, and every one seemed to be mindful of the head master's strict injunction that no one should kill any birds but a bluejay.

All the song-birds were fearless, and rewarded the boys by constant and exquisite music. The hummingbirds were the boys' chief favorites, and early one morning when they found a number of their pets chilled and benumbed on the ground they took them up, administered sugar and water, and when the little creatures had become quite warm, and the genial Californian sun was well up in the sky, they gave them their liberty, and rejoiced to see these brilliant jewels of the air darting thankfully away.

My next experience with a hummingbird was in Canada. During our pleasant summer weather we always had, if in the city, window-boxes full of nasturtiums, and to these boxes several hummingbirds came daily. Whenever we heard the rapid vibration of our brilliant-winged visitors conversation was hushed in the rooms inside.

One summer evening a man brought me a young hummingbird, and said that his cat had caught it, but fortunately he had been able to rescue it before any harm had been done. The little bird was cold and feeble, and taking him in my hand I put his head against my face. After the manner of young hummingbirds with their parents, before they leave the nest, he put his tiny bill into my mouth and thrust out an extremely long and microscopic tongue in search of food.

He soon discovered that he was not with his parents. I had neither honey nor insects for him. However, I did the next best thing, and sent to a druggist for the purest honey that he had. In the meantime, I put my tiny visitor on the window-boxes. The old hummingbirds must have taken all the honey, for he seemed to find nothing there to satisfy him until I put some of that the druggist sent into the blossoms. I held them to his bill and he drank greedily, then, after looking around the room, he flew up to a picture frame, put his head under his wing, and went to sleep.

The next morning at daylight I looked up at the picture. The hummingbird woke up, said "Peep, peep!" a great number of times, in a thin, sweet voice, no louder than a cricket's chirp, but did not come down.

I got up, filled a nasturtium with honey, pinned it to a stick, and held it up to my little visitor, who was charmed to have his breakfast in bed. Finally he condescended to come down, visited other flowers and had more drinks, then I opened the window and told him he was too lovely and too exquisite an occupant for an aviary, and he had better seek his brilliant brothers of the outer air.

He went like a flash of sunshine, and I have never regretted releasing him, for I would rather have had an eagle die on my hands than this tiny, painted beauty. Hummingbirds have been kept in captivity when great care has been exercised in providing for them. A conservatory or hothouse is a good place for them, for there they get the sun's rays which are absolutely essential to their well-being, and they also find on the plants the nearest approach to their natural food.

The objection to this method of keeping these fragile birds is that their delicate frames are quickly injured by coming into contact with hard substances during their rapid flight. The better way is to enclose them inside a mosquito netting stretched on a frame. The best way of all is never to confine them—to give them entire liberty, for of all birds the hummingbird is the least suitable for a life of languishing captivity.

Purple finches have been very favorite pets of mine. Those that I have had have been quiet and amiable, and among the most good-natured and obliging of my birds. The first time I heard them sing I was enraptured. Their song was so sweet, so modest, so melodious. One finch I possessed amused me greatly. He fell into a kind of slavery to a siskin, who followed him and worried him until he at last consented to help her make a nest, in which there were some fine young ones that might have turned out promising hybrids if some wicked, larger bird had not one day killed the neat, determined little mother. I found her headless body beside her nest. She had died in defense of her home. One of the gallinules had probably come along and killed her when she refused to leave her nest.

Her death was a tragedy, but it left the hen-pecked finch free, and he soon devoted himself to his best-loved bird—a female finch of his own class. He adored this shy, second mate—the siskin had been a bold little thing. I often opened the door of the veranda-room for him and sat quietly in a corner while he led in the finch so that they could be away from the rougher birds outside.

Picking up a little bit of wool or hair in his beak the finch would elevate his head-feathers till they almost formed a crest, and would extend his reddish wings and shake them till they looked like a hummingbird's. Then, making a pretty, coaxing noise, he would spin round and round the room in a kind of skirt dance.

The female teased him a good deal by looking the other way and pretending not to see him, but finally he persuaded her to make a nest, where she laid eggs and hatched them, but the young ones only lived a short time—I think because she was shy and easily frightened from them.

She almost fell a victim to another tragedy, for one day, on stepping to the veranda, I found her swinging from a branch by her slender neck. I ran to her, and found that a long hair had become fastened round her neck, and if I had not opportunely appeared she would soon have strangled to death. Fortunately she seemed none the worse for her adventure.

She was a brave little bird, and one habit of hers used to

amuse me immensely. She was a great bather, and enjoyed her baths keenly during mild weather. Unlike many of my birds, who absolutely would not bathe when the cold days came, she kept on, but as if urged to her ablutions by a sense of duty she cried all the time she was bathing.

"Wee, wee!" she would exclaim, as she splashed into the water, then rose up tremblingly, "This water is dreadfully cold, but I must bathe. Wee, wee!" and down she would go again. I kept the aviary quite cool in the winter, but any birds that liked could sit near the hot-water pipes.

Very different from our native finches are the little foreigners of the same name. I am informed that there are thousands and thousands of these tiny foreign finches brought to America from Africa, Asia, and Australia. Some are only two and a half inches long, some are four, few are as large as the average canary.

Many of these finches are bred in captivity, but in most cases they are wild, and are caught by natives with more or less cruelty. Some of the African finches are said to be stupefied by the smoke of fires built under their roosting-places. They drop into blankets spread by the cunning Negroes and are given to captains of vessels in exchange for mock jewelry or rum.

On shipboard they are placed in boxes with wire fronts and their little anxious faces rise tier on tier. The voyage is long, and overcrowding and disease do their work. The wonder is that any survive. Fancy the contrast between the splendors of the African forest and the horrors of this crowded ship!

Upon arriving in America the bird-dealers take the tiny captives in hand, open their filthy cages, put them in clean ones, and exhibit them in their windows.

I do not believe that there is any overpowering desire on the part of the American public to possess these fragile foreigners. However, the bird-dealer must live, and when passers-by see the pale blue, ruby, lavender, or orange-colored little beauties in the windows, they buy them and kindly and ignorantly set about keeping them. Of course, the birds in most cases die, but the Negro goes on getting his rum, the captain gets his money, and the dealer makes a living.

I believe the average person would rather have a canary than a finch. The canary is used to this climate and the finch is not. Why not have all this traffic in caged birds supervised by humane societies? I do not wish to reflect upon the character of all bird-dealers. Many of them are honest men, and some of them I know really love their birds. There are, however, many dealers who are in the business solely to make money, and as long as they are permitted to do as they please, birds will suffer.

Humane societies are not money-making concerns. The members usually consist of the most altruistic citizens of any place. They wish to do what is for the good of their village, town, or city. It would certainly be better for the birds and better for the public to have them regulate this traffic.

I had only two pairs of foreign finches. I would buy no more when I learned how they were captured. The first were cutthroats, and dear little birds they were, so devoted to each other and so surprised to find that the bird world was not full of good little creatures like themselves. When other birds boxed their ears they would fly to each other, rub each other's heads, and murmur consolation.

They were fawn-colored birds, delicately mottled on the breast, with dark-brown spots. The male only had the red stripe across the throat, that gives him his dreadful name. They were very tame, and often while I stood close to them the male, as if struck by a sudden thought, would jump up, dance up and down on his tiny feet, turning his body from side to side as he did so, and sing a hoarse little song. The song and dance were so comical that I frequently burst out laughing, but his feelings never seemed hurt, and he soon broke out again.

In the intervals between his dancing he would press close to his diminutive mate—she was much smaller than a canary—and carried on his favorite occupation of gently rubbing her head with his beak. Once, when she was struck by a large bird, I saw her fly right to him, and it was very pretty to observe the intensely affectionate, sympathetic way in which he went all over her head with his tiny beak, as if to say, "Which is the sore place?—let me rub it for you."

They were so devoted to each other that they invariably kept together when flying from one part of the aviary to the other, so that one day I was surprised to see them separated. I looked about and found that they had made a nest over some hot-water pipes. These little birds are very prolific, and hatch young ones freely in captivity. A lady is reported to have had from one pair in three years, as many as forty-five broods—altogether over two hundred and forty eggs, from which one hundred and seventy-six were hatched. I hoped very much that I might have some tiny cutthroats, but the nest was in too warm a place, and the eggs did not amount to anything.

A new bird, on going into an aviary, usually chooses a pet place for sleeping and resting, and keeps to it. The little cutthroats chose their place in some fir trees near the doves. The doves pushed them about a little, but the cutthroats soon learned to avoid them.

The only birds that conquered the doves were the Java sparrows. These sparrows are nice little birds, but I never had a high opinion of their intelligence, until I saw how they dominated these same stubborn doves.

They never bothered the doves in summer, but every winter the Javas persisted in sleeping between them on cold nights. On going into the aviary after dark, I would see one Java tucked between the doves, and another on the outside of one of them.

The clever little things had discovered that the doves'

bodies were warm and comforting. I was puzzled to know how they maintained their footing, for the doves gave resounding slaps of their wings to any little bird who went too near them.

One night I discovered the Javas' trick. When the dove lifted its wing to strike, the Java slipped under it and missed the force of the blow. After a time the dove got tired of beating, and the Java went to sleep. There were many other birds in the aviary, but the Javas never attempted to sleep near any of them but the ringdoves or the white doves.

After I had had Father Cutthroat nearly a year, he vanished mysteriously, and poor Mrs. Cutthroat in her desolation behaved very badly. She would slyly watch my Bengalese finches—two other tiny birds that looked like fawn and white butterflies—and as soon as they made a nest she would drive them from it, and lay eggs herself in the usurped place.

This excited the Bengalese birds. The male would dance up and down and sing his little song that sounded like, "Hardly able, set the table; hardly able, set the table!" But if he approached the nest, Widow Cutthroat would rise, lean over the edge, sway to and fro, and make a hissing noise like a little snake.

In spite of her apparent devotion to a particular nest, she never kept to it, and as soon as the Bengalese pair made a new one, she would take it from them. I excused her bad conduct on the plea that she was grieving over the loss of her devoted mate. Where could he be? I looked high and low in the aviary below, and the roof-veranda above—if he were dead I would at least find his body. It was impossible for him to escape through the fine wire netting.

Finally, his body or skeleton did appear, in a sudden and unexpected manner. It was immediately below the box of my flying-squirrels. These squirrels had been in the aviary for a long time. They were beautiful little creatures with soft, silky fur and very large eyes. I had got them with the intention of

taming them but, unfortunately, they only came out of their box at night. I often went in and looked long and earnestly at them as they ran and jumped about searching for food, but I did not attempt to play with them as I would have disturbed my sleeping birds.

Their favorite haunt was, of course, the roof-veranda, but I soon found out that they could not sail horizontally, but only downward. A favorite sport with them is to run to the top, of a tree, flying down to the near-by branches of a lower one, run to the top of this, and then fly down to another. Jumping or springing squirrels would really be a better name for them.

They were very quiet in their movements, and I do not think the birds minded them any more than they did the few mice that I could not keep out of the aviary. The mice were really very amusing, as they crept quietly from place to place, searching for the scraps of food the birds had left. They were not afraid of me, and I often smiled as I held up my lantern and saw them climbing over tree trunks and branches, as naturally as if they too were birds, and occasionally stopping short, and peering at me with their beady eyes.

I guessed that the cutthroat had been exploring, and in searching for a new place for a nest had been led by his curiosity to enter the squirrels' open doorway. Resenting the intrusion, they had probably jumped at him and killed him. I knew that red squirrels would kill birds, and being now suspicious of these gray gymnasts, I had a carpenter come and fasten their box outside instead of inside the netting. Naturally, they did not stay in it, and I hope ran either to the gardens or the park, where they would find numbers of red squirrels to play with them.

CHAPTER XXVIII

JAPANESE ROBINS AND A BOBOLINK

I have not up to this time said much about the birds in my collection that were usually most remarked by strangers. They were the Japanese robins, or Peking nightingales.

I had heard of these red-billed, orange-breasted little birds with their large black eyes, and shortly after I began keeping birds had one sent to me. He was indeed a beauty, and in excellent condition, and had traveled as comfortably as a bird can travel in a good-sized cage with plenty of food and a sponge in his drinking-cup, so that if the water were spilt, he could suck the moisture from it.

I took him into my study, and in trying to slip him from his traveling-cage into a larger one, for I always like to keep new arrivals in quarantine for a few days, he escaped from me.

Now I was to see some of the lightning-like movements that the bird books spoke of. I closed the doors and he went around the room like a streak of light. I thoroughly believed what I had heard—that no cat can catch this robin, unless he chooses to be caught, and that he can clear a room of flies in a few minutes. Now he was this side of me, now the other. I had to keep turning my head to follow the swift motions of this little acrobat. As I watched him I admired more and more the red and orange of his costume, and the ring of white around his wonderful eyes that gave him a distinguished and foreign appearance. I had read of his rich, throaty song, his mellow calls, and listened anxiously for the first sounds to issue from his pretty throat.

To my dismay he suddenly began to scold me, uttering hoarse, chattering, grating noises. I saw that he was excited and angry. This was not singing. It was scolding. I put him in the aviary the next day, and stopped staring at him. He hid for some time in a fir tree, then he came out, began to be at home, never acted shy or strange again, and sang nearly all day long a song that was all my fancy had imagined it.

I was intensely interested in this foreigner that never for an instant lost his foreign look, his foreign ways, and yet who seemed more at home than any native bird in my aviary. He kept up his inconceivably yet gracefully rapid movements. He would start at one end of the aviary, snatch a morsel from a food-dish, peck at a bit of fruit, turn a kind of somersault in the air, and land in a water-pan, where he would take a partial bath, and then dart off again. I never saw him take a complete bath, though he would be in the tub forty times a day. He was always in too much of a hurry to finish.

He seemed to have quite a talent for mischief, and one day I could not help smiling as I saw him play a roguish trick on my robin Bob. He watched her leave her nest and get out of sight, then he darted to the eggs, settled down on them with a blissful expression of countenance and shut his eyes, as if to say, "How lovely to have something to care for!" Another flash of thought then struck him. He sprang up, gave one of the eggs a good sharp peck that made a hole in it, and scampered off to avoid reprisals from the wrathful Bob who screamed if any one meddled with her eggs.

Nearly all the time this robin flew about the aviary he kept up a gurgling, blissful song, and so fascinated was I with him that I sent away for a mate. She soon came. I had found a bird-dealer who really seemed to love his birds, and who never sent me a poor one or a sick one. When Mrs. Jap arrived, my friend, the first bird, nearly lost his head. I have said that when I got him he went around the room like a streak of lightning. If it were possible for one to see two streaks in one I now was the favored individual.

He, the enterprising happy bird, had been living as a stranger in a strange land. Here now was a beloved little sister, right from his own dear land. What was he to do about it? Intense joy so urged him on that he could not stop long enough to speak to her. The fastidious, exquisite little female, in the intervals of cleaning her plumage, disarranged by travel, kept calling to him in a voice as rich as his own, "Where, oh where, oh where are you, my dear, oh!

"Here I am, oh! here I am, oh! here I am, oh!" he would respond like a melodious flashlight, and finally he sobered down and she, having finished her toilet, began to fly with him. From that day to this they have been inseparable companions, chasing each other's bright wings about the aviary, bathing, eating, drinking—not together usually, but one after the other in a hurried, graceful fashion. One amusing trick they had was to fly swiftly by my head and brush my ears with the tips of their wings.

When tired of playing, singing, and eating, they occasionally settled down for a nap. I used to think they were fast asleep, when lo! the male would wake up with a start, as if he had forgotten something, and would begin to rub his companion's head with his red bill. The female also woke up, turning her head round and round for him to shampoo every part of it, then after he had finished she did her duty by going over his head.

At night they used to sleep close beside each other, and always raised their pretty heads when I went near them with my lantern. They were never afraid of being captured, for I did not have to doctor them or handle them in any way. They had excellent appetites, and the immense amount of exercise they took kept them in fine condition.

They were never vicious birds, but sometimes they exhibited a mischievous inclination to chase the smaller inhabitants of the aviary. I never knew them to kill a bird, except the aggravating yellow warbler.

When I left home this autumn I pondered long over my duty toward these two beauties. I had had them for some years, and they had thoroughly explored my aviary, darting about the lower one, soaring up the elevator, around the roof-veranda, and down again. They liked me, but had no real love for me as some of my birds seemed to have. So, knowing that they could be happy elsewhere, and knowing also that I could not leave too many birds at home, I chose these two happy, debonair creatures for exile.

I sent them to the kind curator of a large aviary, where I hear they are perfectly well and happy, as I knew they would be. Long may they live! No brighter, smarter little bird exists than the Japanese robin.

A very dear little bird that I had in my aviary was a bobolink. He was a sober-looking bird when I got him, for he was in his winter dress—yellowish brown with dusky wings and tail. When spring came he blossomed out into a new suit with trimmings of cream and white—and how he sang! I never had a bird that took more pleasure in his own society. He would get by himself in a corner, safely out of the way of quarrels, and sing a captivating tangle of song, till he was exhausted and had to refresh himself by a hearty meal.

He ate and drank and sang, and every time I think of him I call up a picture of a pretty bird leaning forward with distended throat from which issues a flood of melody.

I loved my dear Bob o'Lincoln, and found out all I could about him. I was delighted to hear that there was a law against the capture of this gayest of songsters, and was interested to know that his kind has quite a wide range—from Utah to Nova Scotia, and from Manitoba to the Amazon. Bobolinks like the North in summer, but sensibly prefer the South in winter, where they have the name of reedbirds or ricebirds. Exasperated farmers down South shoot poor Bob because he and his numerous progeny stuff themselves in fields of rice and oats. However, if it were not for Bob and other insectivorous birds, the grain might never ripen, for in the spring and summer they must subsist largely on the insects that are worse enemies of man than are the birds.

I kept Bob a year or two. The second summer I had him on my farm I listened one day to the wild bobolinks down in the meadow, pouring out their bird hearts in delicious harmonies, then I opened the door of the room where Bob was and recommended him to join those merry fellows in the alders by the river. He sat for an hour or two as if deliberating, then he flew off in a leisurely way, and I saw him no more, but I know quite well that he would join his wild cousins, and when the autumn came, would fly south with them.

I have several other birds in mind that I should like to write about, but I think the story of my pets is already long enough. I shall be satisfied if I have made birds a little more interesting to persons who already love them, and if I cause a few to become interested, who have cared nothing for them. They are exquisite creatures, and the more one studies them the more he finds to admire in them, and the greater number of points of resemblance are there discovered between them and human beings.

There are cruel birds and kind birds, intelligent birds and stupid birds—birds that perhaps do not converse, but that certainly communicate to each other impressions and sensations in a kind of language of their own, and birds that scarcely converse at all. Yet after all, their intelligence is not our intelligence. One gets birds to a certain point, and they go no farther. However, they are eminently suitable as friends and companions for man.

Why is it that we have been so cruel to them? Why is it that the first thought of a bird in the mind of a boy is usually associated with the thought of a gun? Our little brothers and sisters of the air were created for us. They ask only for the privilege of toiling unremittingly for us. Their busy little beaks are from morning till night at the service of their brother man.

We have got to learn better how to appreciate their services. If we do not, there are dark days in store for this nation, for if the birds perish from the face of the earth naturalists tell us that man will perish too.

There are three things we must do—we must take energetic measures to protect, first, our children; secondly, our birds; and thirdly, our forests.

Statisticians tell us that industrial slavery is ruining many children who should become healthy mothers and fathers of families. They also tell us that the lack of protection of insect-eating birds is taking from the pockets of this nation every year the almost inconceivable sum of eight hundred millions of dollars, and that the present frightful waste of wood if not checked, will cause us to be without timber, outside the national forests, in from twenty to forty years.

What are we going to do about it?

Are we to sink still further into the gross, short-sighted materialism of our age, or are we to wish for an awakening and quickening of the old American spirit—the spirit of one small shipload of persons that was, however, strong enough at one time to dominate this continent?

"We are our brothers' keepers," said our stern and honest Pilgrim ancestors. "We are our brothers' keepers," we, their children, must learn to echo—keepers even to the beasts of the field and to our little brothers and sisters of the air, that have a right to exist and to lead their own lives, and to demand from us created beings of a higher order protection, sympathy, and goodfellowship.

www.ingramcontent.com/pod-product-compliance
Lightning Source LLC
LaVergne TN
LVHW040012200726
843493LV00005B/1239